Andrew Carnegie
and the
Rise of Big Business

Harold C. Livesay

Texas A&M University

Andrew Carnegie
and the
Rise of Big Business

Second Edition

Edited by Oscar Handlin

147727

An imprint of Addison Wesley Longman, Inc.

New York • Reading, Massachusetts • Menlo Park, California • Harlow, England
Don Mills, Ontario • Sydney • Mexico City • Madrid • Amsterdam

Acquisitions Editor: Jay O'Callaghan
Executive Marketing Manager: Sue Westmoreland
Project Manager: Donna DeBenedictis
Design Manager/Text Designer: John Callahan
Cover Designer: Kay Petronio
Cover Photo: Andrew Carnegie. Oil on canvas. 127.6 x 101.9 cm.
   (50¼ x 40⅛ in.) National Portrait Gallery, Smithsonian Institution.
Photo Researcher: Mira Schachne
Electronic Production Specialist: Sarah Johnson
Senior Print Buyer: Hugh Crawford
Electronic Page Makeup: Sarah Johnson
Printer and Binder: RR Donnelley & Sons Company/Harrisonburg
Cover Printer: Phoenix Color Corp

Brief extracts appear in the book that are taken from *The Autobiography of Andrew Carnegie*. New York: Houghton Mifflin, 1920. Copyright renewed 1948 by Margaret Carnegie Miller.

Illustrations: *Frontispiece and pages 2, 14, 28, 44, 60, 108, 130, and 146:* Brown Brothers; *page 76: Harper's Weekly,* April 10, 1886; *pages 92 and 168:* Compix/UPI/Corbis-Bettmann.

Library of Congress Cataloging-in-Publication Data
Livesay, Harold C.
   Andrew Carnegie and the rise of big business / Harold C. Livesay ;
edited by Oscar Handlin.—2nd ed.
      p.   cm.—(Library of American biography series)
   Includes bibliographical references and index.
   ISBN 0-321-04373-1 (pbk.)
   1. Carnegie, Andrew, 1835–1919. 2. Industrialists—United States
Biography. 3. Millionaires—United States Biography. 4. Philanthropists—
United States Biography. 5. Steel industry and trade—United States—
History. 6. Iron industry and trade—United States—History. 7. Big
business—United States—History. I. Handlin, Oscar, 1915–   . II. Title.
III. Series: Library of American biography (New York, N.Y.)
HD9520.C3L58   1999
338.7'672'092—dc21   99-33825
[B]   CIP

Please visit our website at http://www.awlonline.com

ISBN 0-321-04373-1

345678910—DOH—020100

For
Earl Scruggs, banjoist
Bill Cosby, philosopher
Thomas Carlyle, historian
and
Mark Harris, professor and novelist

They taught me that
there is more to the truth
than facts

Contents

Editor's Preface

The term "industrial revolution" has become a catch phrase that obscures rather than clarifies. All too often it conveys the impression that the economic process which transformed the modern world began with an event at some point in eighteenth-century England, from which all subsequent consequences proceeded smoothly and continuously.

The actuality was far more complex. The basic changes stretched over two hundred years and are not yet over. They involved not only the new technology of machines, but also profound alterations in the organization of work and in habits of the mind.

Andrew Carnegie exemplified one phase of the change. He arrived in the United States at a crucial moment in its development. When the small boy Andy and his family left Scotland, British industrialization was well underway; indeed, their migration resulted from one of its unexpected consequences. When the Carnegies reached Pittsburgh, Americans had already begun to move in the same direction; the founding of the early manufacturing mills at Lowell, Massachusetts, was decades past. Significantly, Carnegie's first job was as a bobbin boy in a textile mill. But both countries had taken only the first hesitant steps in industrialization. Manufacturing was still primarily a rural activity and still small in scale.

Carnegie was involved in reorganizing the whole pattern of industrial activity. Early in his career he changed jobs, moving from textiles to the telegraph office and then to the railroads. Those shifts were symbolic insofar as they brought him into contact with the dynamic forces that were altering communications and were creating large regional economic units to replace the earlier, small ones. Much of what he learned about communications and transportation he later ingeniously adapted to the steel industry.

Carnegie also exemplified the habits of mind important at one stage of industrial development. He was a Scot, a fact most clearly manifest in the ethnic links that helped at each point in his career. He showed the capacity to use capital and technicians well, not in a speculative or an exploitive fashion, but to create wealth. That he remained apart from the corporate developments commonly associated with the closing decade of the nineteenth century—as, indeed, did his contemporary Andrew W. Mellon—was not an accident. When he finally sold out to United States Steel, he closed his own career and also the stage of development in which he had actively participated. By then, however, as Harold C. Livesay's book shows, Carnegie had helped to establish the foundations of American economic power.

Oscar Handlin

Acknowledgments

The author of a book as long in print as this one acquires many debts. Without series editor Oscar Handlin, whose deft touch pared away my excesses, the book could never have succeeded so well. Jay O'Callaghan, who has managed to retain a personal touch in an era of impersonalization of the publishing industry, supplied the needed encouragement to undertake the revision.

I owe a special debt of gratitude to the hundreds of colleagues and students who have written over the years to say they found the book useful; I wrote it for them, and their enjoyment has provided a particularly gratifying reward. A wholly unexpected bonus has come from the many people who told me they found Carnegie's maxims the most valuable component of their own success. I hope the new edition will continue to serve as the old one has.

Harold C. Livesay

Andrew Carnegie

and the
Rise of Big Business

From rags to richest: top, the weaver's cottage in Dunfermline, Scotland, where Andrew Carnegie was born; bottom, Skibo Castle, his home in Scotland later in life

I

Flying Scots:
In Search of a Dream

Nothing has characterized America more than the "American dream"—the enduring belief that people can rise above their origins, however humble, and through hard work, honesty, and thrift achieve positions of power and influence, even the presidency of the United States. The dream evolved logically from the aspirations of the early settlers. Whether they came seeking freedom from established churches or liberation from the social and economic strictures of postfeudal European societies, the restless, ambitious people who populated the New World found in its natural wealth, gentle climate, and seemingly endless land an arena in which to strive for their goals. In colonial America ex-convicts sometimes did become land owners; former indentured servants occasionally did become successful businessmen. By the time the republic achieved its independence from Great Britain, the once faint hope that poor men might find a better life in America had transformed into a viable tradition one hundred and fifty years old.

Throughout the nineteenth century the dream was attested to by the letters of aristocratic émigrés such as the farmer St. John de Crèvecoeur and the manufacturer Irénée duPont, publicized by foreign observers such as Alexis de Tocqueville, reinforced by the election of presidents born in log cabins, and given credence above all by the letters and money sent by thousands of immigrants to anxious families and friends in the homeland. The American dream thus became one of the impulses propelling the migration of tens of millions from the Old World to the New. From these multitudes some men rose to wealth and power equal to their wildest dreams. Of course the Guggenheims and Vanderbilts were always a tiny minority, but enough of them appeared and their successes were trumpeted so widely that the dream became permanently embedded in folklore at home and in the country's image abroad.

Wars, depressions, and the evils of industrialization have not driven the dream from the American consciousness. It permeates social commentary at the turn of the twenty-first century as it did in the nineteenth, even though some present-day observers, noting the failure of capitalism to eradicate poverty and its tendency to widen the gap between rich and poor, may dwell on the disappointments of American life as much as on its successes. These critics view the dream largely in terms of its shortcomings: the staggering environmental costs of headlong industrialization; the painful social costs of urban squalor and rural poverty; the systematic exclusion of blacks, women, and other groups from equal enjoyment of the benefits of the system. The abuses draw as much attention as the individual success stories; yet even the vehemence of the criticism testifies to the tenacity of the tradition. Most Americans still believe that a man—and increasingly, a woman—can rise or, at the very least, that one's children can, and anecdotal supporting evidence continues to accumulate: Roberto Goizueta emigrated from Cuba to the United States in 1960 with $40 in his pocket, rose to the chairmanship of Coca-Cola, and increased the company's value from $3 billion to $152 billion by the time he died in 1997; Andy Grove survived Hitler and Stalin, fled from Hungary to the United States, waited tables to put himself through college, built Intel into the corporation whose chips power 85 percent of the world's personal computers, and was named *Time* magazine's man of the year for 1997; Liz Claiborne started as a clothing design assistant in the early 1950s, created her own firm in 1976, which went on to revolutionize the American women's fashion industry and become the number one "star" of the *Fortune* "500"'s "Return on Equity, 1979–1988" list. Stories such as Goizueta's, Grove's, and Claiborne's have kept alive the legend that Carnegie's story did so much to validate.

Andrew Carnegie's rise from poor Scottish immigrant boy to "the richest man in the world" seemed to his contemporaries and to succeeding generations irrefutable evidence of the dream's validity. For this reason alone his career deserves examination, but there are even more compelling grounds for investigating his life in detail. Many of Carnegie's attitudes reflected ideas widely accepted among Americans. He thought that machines were a blessing, not a curse, that individual success improved society as a whole and demonstrated progress, and that the American political system made possible the spectacular growth of industrial economy. Yet he himself personified many of the paradoxes that beset his adopted country. He espoused the creed of rugged individualism, but did much to usher in the era of impersonal corporate bureaucracy; he publicly advocated and often practiced the doctrine of free enterprise in business, but supported protective tariffs, sometimes joined pools, and finally sold out to a combine expressly formed to eliminate competition in the steel industry.

Carnegie also merits attention because he perfected business techniques that reshaped the iron and steel industry. He entered this old field at the head of a new firm, which he organized and operated according to management principles he had learned on the railroad. By adhering determinedly to these modern methods, and by driving his profits back into the business in expanded facilities and updated equipment, Carnegie transformed the iron and steel industry from a diffuse assortment of small producers into the nation's first manufacturing "big business." By the end of the nineteenth century Carnegie had built his firm into a modern giant that produced more steel than the entire British industry and did it so cheaply that no competitor could match his price. Firms in other industries adapted Carnegie's techniques to fit their own managerial needs. He thus played a crucial role in formulating the systems of industrial management that controlled and coordinated the spectacular economic growth of late-nineteenth-century America. The principles on which he based his management system long survived him, and one of them, that continued profitability depends on an obsession with cost control, keyed the resurgence of American industry, including the American steel industry, in the 1990s.

This remarkable career, which did so much to advertise and authenticate the American dream, certainly began in modest and commonplace circumstances when, on July 15, 1848, the sailing ship *Wiscasset,* fifty days out of Glasgow, deposited its cargo of immigrants at Castle Garden in New York harbor, an event that drew no notice, for at the time upwards of forty passenger ships a day dropped anchor in New York harbor, laden with hopeful additions to the New World. As the Carnegies debarked, other little-noticed events with noteworthy future consequences unfolded elsewhere in America: Brigham Young and 143 Mormon followers trudged along on the last leg of their trek to the Great Salt Lake Basin; feminists

Elizabeth Cady Stanton and Lucretia Mott, together with a group of sympathizers male and female, had convened the first women's rights convention at Seneca Falls, New York.

The four Carnegies, Will and Margaret and their children, Andrew and Tom, differed little from the *Wiscasset*'s other steerage passengers; indeed, little distinguished them from the 150,000 other immigrants who arrived from Great Britain in that year. Tired from the long trip in cramped quarters, weak from poor food and lack of exercise, poor, with no money to spare, the Carnegies shared with their fellow Scottish passengers a hope that the new country would offer what the old had denied: the chance to make a decent living and restore the self-respect that years of little or no employment had sapped.

Like many other immigrants, the Carnegies had relatives in America. Mrs. Carnegie's sisters, Annie Aitken and Kitty Hogan, had migrated with their husbands in 1840. In the intervening years the Hogans and the Aitkens had written home often, the tone of their letters rising or falling with the economic fortunes of their new homeland. In good times Annie Aitken extolled America as "far better for the working man. In fact you seem to breathe a freer atmosphere here." She also emphasized the more favorable position enjoyed by women in America where "men . . . seem so anxious to let them have an easy life." In bad times their relatives urged the Carnegies to stay home, and lamented their own departure:

> My dear Margaret, . . . it would be the height of folly to advise you [to come] as it is difficult . . . to get employment of any kind . . . particularly weaving which is hardly carried out here at all. [1840]

> I wish I had . . . not come to America this soon—the banking system has made sad havoc . . . business is at a stand. . . . [1842]

> I would not advise any person to come . . . who can get a live-
> ly hood at home, as trade is very dull here, indeed many who
> are both willing & able to work find it impossible to get
> employment. [1842]

Faced with such mixed reports, the Carnegies clung to
Scotland as long as they could despite their dwindling fortunes. They finally left because conditions at home became
intolerable, not because opportunities abroad were irresistible. The presence of relatives and the apparently glim-
mering opportunities made the United States a natural destination. If the Carnegies could have stayed in Scotland,
they would have, regardless of the lure from across the
ocean; and Andrew, who became the apotheosis of the
American dream, might instead have become part of the
folklore of his native Scotland.

Andrew Carnegie was born on November 25, 1835, in
Dunfermline, fourteen miles north of Edinburgh.
Although it was the largest town in County Fife,
Dunfermline had a rural setting; it was surrounded by hills
and glens, and overlooked the Firth of Forth. Andrew
spent his boyhood among ruins and relics of Scotland's
history—Dunfermline Abbey, Malcolm's Tower, multiple
monuments to Mary Queen of Scots, the palace and tomb
of King Robert the Bruce—and among relatives who
delighted in spinning tales about them. In particular his
uncle George Lauder introduced him to the legends of
William Wallace and King Robert the Bruce, the plays of
Shakespeare, the ballads of Scotland, and above all, the
poetry of Robert Burns. The boy also learned about the
United States and its heroes—Washington, Jefferson,
Franklin—and the greatness of the society they and their
successors had built. Andrew embraced his uncle's enthusiasms, including pacifism and a Radical view of politics.
Later he cited him as "the man to whom I owe most, and
who was nearest and dearest to me . . . my uncle and
father, for such he was since I reached manhood."

Carnegie's time and place of birth exposed him not only to historical reliquiae and troubadours of Scottish legendry, but to the ferment of contemporary politics as well, for Dunfermline had long been "renowned as perhaps the most radical town in the kingdom," according to Carnegie. In 1838 the town's leading Radicals—Carnegie's father and maternal uncle Will Morrison among them—became Chartists, that is, advocates of parliamentary enactment of the People's Charter. The Charter, first published by the London Working Men's Association in 1838, demanded six concessions: universal manhood suffrage, the secret ballot, annual elections of Parliament, equal electoral districts, the removal of property qualifications for election to Parliament, and payment for members of Parliament, to enable others besides the rich to hold office.

Throughout his boyhood Carnegie heard his father and Uncle Morrison speak for the Charter at public rallies and listened to discussions at home about strategies to achieve its adoption; he shared the family's anxiety when his Uncle Morrison was arrested in 1842 for the "seditious activity" of inciting a general strike in Dunfermline to support the Charter. Andrew imbibed the principles of the Charter and swallowed whole the utopian claims of its supporters that it would cure all of society's ills: "Political equality, that is all we ask, and then everything else will follow: the prosperous yeoman, the respected artisan, the happy child. Give us the Charter and we can take care of ourselves."

Throughout his life Carnegie clung to his belief that the lack of political equality lay at the heart of his mother country's social and economic woes, causing the conditions that forced his family to leave Scotland. In his later years he realized that Dunfermline's economy had collapsed not because most of its citizens could not vote, but because their incomes depended on an anachronistic trade. He remained convinced, however, that political reform could have tempered the social consequences of economic progress.

Dunfermline's livelihood depended on the hand weaving of linen, an honored craft practiced by half of its 11,000 inhabitants. In 1835 the town's weavers still engaged in an art essentially unchanged since its medieval origins. The changes that had come—largely improvements to the loom—had been designed to reinforce the weavers' skills, not to supplant them. But the very qualities that made linen weaving so special a craft—the large amount of labor, time, and skill required to produce each piece—rendered the trade particularly susceptible to machine competition. By the time Carnegie was born, such competition had already devastated many branches of the traditional textile trades and communities in Europe. The linen industry of Dunfermline soon felt the same shattering force.

The shift to machine production (the Industrial Revolution) resulted from an energy revolution (first achieved in England) in which steam boilers replaced windmills, waterwheels, animals, and men as power sources for manufacturing. Dependent on the weather, windmills and waterwheels were unreliable; men and animals, dependent on food crops, requiring regular rest, and converting energy slowly, were inefficient. Steam boilers, however, could be run almost continuously on coal, which in England was abundant and accessible in all weathers. Their introduction thus unlocked a new store of potential energy, so enormous, so powerful that it often inspired contemporary observers to allude to Vulcan, Tubal Cain, and Hell itself in their efforts to construct adequately evocative metaphors.

Coal-fired boilers generated more than literary enthusiasms. English capitalists, engineers, and mechanics, who had learned the relationship of heat, energy, and work from Isaac Newton's principles of thermodynamics, quickly realized that the new power sources promised to multiply geometrically the output of existing industry and to open whole new fields to profitable exploitation. This in turn led to visions of vast benefits. Industrialization would expand national income (then a novel idea, stagnation being more familiar than growth), produce more goods for overseas trade, and strengthen the nation's ability to defend itself and its empire. (The English had been supporting defense industries for centuries, notably shipyards, firearms manufactories, and cannon foundries. The relationship of industrial capacity to military power was not lost on them.) But most important, industrialization offered a basic solution to poverty and unemployment, problems from which England had long suffered.

The problem of the poor had been inescapable in an agrarian economy. The indigent and unemployed had constantly drained away the benefits of the greater production that crop rotation, soil improvement, field and fen drainage, and fertilization coaxed out of English farms. Population, as Parson Malthus was gloomily to observe, tended to expand as fast as agricultural production; moreover, some of the increased output stemmed from farming practices that often intensified the problem of unemployment. A shift from labor-intensive arable farming to sheep and cattle raising sometimes left men jobless, as did enclosure, the combining of many small farms into a few large ones, with or without the smallholders' consent. Rising farm output thus brought more food but did not alleviate unemployment. Moreover, no matter how much capital might be invested in clearing and draining land, or in increasing crop yields through soil improvement, hybrid development, and mechanization, sooner or later the finite quantity of land meant that diminishing returns had to set in. By the end of the eighteenth century, many suspected that the time would come (it did shortly) when British farmers, however efficient, could not feed their own population. The populace would face starvation and a stagnant economy if it remained tied to agriculture as its primary source of income.

Manufacturing offered solutions to all these problems. Factories could not create food as such (though they could make machines that helped grow it), but they generated goods that could be sold overseas for food. Moreover, although land cannot reproduce itself, machines can; factories might be multiplied indefinitely, increasing national income, absorbing the unemployed, transforming them into self-supporting, useful citizens. Their imaginations fired with these glowing prospects of national prosperity, personal wealth, and social uplift, the British drove the engine of industrialization forward. Powered by merchants' and landowners' capital, implemented by great engineers (Bolton, Watt, Trevethick, Telford, the Stephensons, Brunel), it steamrolled those among the gentry and the poets who objected. Because the benefits were more manifest than the drawbacks, the latter could be justified as the unavoidable but bargain price. After all, if the machine brought progress and a panacea for the country's ills, then any cost seemed affordable.

As it turned out, industrialization did all that its supporters had promised. British national income multiplied from £48 million in 1688 to £1.6 billion in 1901 as Britain became the world's foremost industrial power, pouring out products to the world; money and machines kept it among the leading military powers. In time, the factories did absorb the British workforce (and much of the Irish one as well) at a rising standard of living, despite the growth of the population from 5.8 million in 1701 to 32.5 million in 1901.

Industrialization cost more than Britain expected, however—the cost was a whole way of life. The factories destroyed the old world of the land, the domain of the farmer and the artisan, and replaced it with the new world of the machine, the domain of mindless factory toil and child labor. In the long run would come national prosperity, trade unions, the Labour Party, and factory legislation; in the short run came wealth for the few and such periods as the "hungry forties" of unemployment, starvation, family disintegration, and dislocation for the many.

The Carnegies were among those whose way of life succumbed to the disorientations generated by machines. The family's debacle came swiftly. In 1836 Will Carnegie had had such a prosperous year that he moved his family to a bigger house, bought three additional looms, and took on apprentices to work them. Just two years later, the decline in prices and demand set in, never to reverse. In 1843 a power loom mill opened in Dunfermline, and Will Carnegie never again found steady employment. Margaret Carnegie eked out the family income by cobbling and opening a small store in the front room of the house. One by one the idle looms were sold. Finally, in the winter of 1847, Will told his son, "Andra, I can get nae mair work."

Ten years thus virtually eradicated Will Carnegie's and Dunfermline's principal source of income, an occupation practiced in the town for three centuries with little change in organization, method, or product. The flow of goods from raw material to finished product was directed by the merchants who, although they were known as "manufacturers," only bought and sold, whereas the various stages of production—spinning, weaving, bleaching, dyeing— were assigned to local craftsmen who carried the work home. Like the organization, the work itself had changed little except for a gradual shift from coarse linen to fine damask as the looms and the weavers' skills improved.

As in most communities long organized around one traditional industry, Dunfermline had a stable social structure. People behaved in established ways and expected others to do the same. Could a seventeenth-century Dunfermline weaver have returned to walk the streets in

1836, he would instantly have recognized the town, its people, and their work. The cobbled streets, the stone cottages of the weavers, the appearance of the weavers themselves, the bobbins of thread and webs of cloth they carried to and from their looms—all these would have seemed familiar, looking as they had in 1736 or even 1636. An old, familiar, stable world this was, in which a man worked at home among his family, quit at nightfall, and raised his sons to expect the same. So Will Carnegie raised Andrew, until the steam looms came. By 1847 it was clear there would be no·trade for the boy to follow. The town and its people adjusted as best they could. Some men worked as laborers on the railway; some found jobs in the steam mill; some sank in despair; and some moved on.

All over Scotland and England, wherever the steam mills appeared, it was the same: customary social patterns shattered as traditional trades collapsed. Just as Dunfermline might have stood for a hundred other dying towns, so also might the Carnegies have represented the 267,000 fellow citizens who gave up and sailed to America in the hungry forties. They sailed reluctantly, desperately, leaving not because the new home promised so much, but because the old home no longer promised anything at all.

On May 17, 1848, the Carnegies left the decay of Dunfermline for a fresh start in the New World. The father Will, weary at forty-three, was emasculated by his own failures and by his wife's determination. The mother Margaret, thirty-three, burned with shame at her husband's failure and despair, shame at leaving in defeat and poverty, shame at having to sell out, beg, and borrow to get passage money. Yet she was also determined to see her sons succeed where their father had failed, determined to return someday in triumph. The elder son Andrew, thirteen, sensing his father's failure and his mother's contempt for it, shared her resolve to recoup the family's losses, and bore in his mind a heady mixture of undigested historical romanticism and political dogma, his philosophical heritage from the old world now left behind. With this anachronistic legacy he soon confronted in America the problems associated with the new industrial world. Only the younger son Tom, five, "a beautiful white-haired child with lustrous black eyes, who everywhere attracted attention," set sail with a mind unburdened by the past.

Because Andrew's lifetime spanned two worlds, before and after mechanization, his actions continuously manifested an ambivalence rooted in his double exposure to the old world among the cottages, glens, and firths of Scotland and the new world of smoky factories in America. Most of his actions as a businessman demonstrated mastery of the techniques of investment, management, technological improvement, and marketing, and of such economic principles as returns to scale and elasticity of demand that formed the core of modern industrial practice. On the other hand, his attitudes toward politics, society, culture, and, curiously enough, even the ownership structure of his business exhibited the Old World ideas he had absorbed as a boy in Scotland.

Andrew Carnegie at sixteen years (left), with his brother Thomas, age eight, photographed in 1851

I I

The Climb Begins

Two years after arriving in America the Carnegie family had rebuilt their fortunes: they enjoyed a total income greater than they had ever known in Scotland; they had repaid the borrowed passage money; and they had bought a house in Allegheny, Pennsylvania. In later life, Andrew's story of the first years in America emphasized the dirt, hard work, and privations. The element of truth in and the popular appeal of that version obscured the fact that the family received vital assistance from relatives, former neighbors, and fellow countrymen from the day of their arrival in New York. Indeed, the Carnegies, like many of their fellow immigrants, counted from the outset on the help of their expatriated countrymen and planned their journey to take advantage of it.

In the nineteenth century, whole ethnic communities grew up around a few hardy souls who ventured from home, established a foothold in the new country, and then reached back to help friends and relatives. In this way, many ethnic neighborhoods became surrogates for villages in Ireland, Scotland, and Germany. When the Carnegies planned their trip, Andrew's mother wrote to her two

sisters and received "satisfactory letters . . . in reply."
When they landed in New York, the James Sloane family
welcomed them. Sloane had worked as a Dunfermline
weaver himself (later he became one of New York's
wealthiest merchants), and Mrs. Sloane was a girlhood
friend of Margaret Carnegie. When the Carnegies reached
Pittsburgh—after a three-week inland voyage that took
them north on the Hudson River to Albany, west on the
Erie Canal, Mohawk River, and Lake Erie to Buffalo and
Cleveland, south and east on the Ohio Canal to Akron and
Beaver Falls, Pennsylvania, then upstream on the Ohio
River to their destination—Mrs. Carnegie's sisters welcomed them joyously. Moreover, Annie Aitken provided
them with rent-free living quarters in a small house she
owned.

The family at once set out to find work (except for Tom,
sent off to school), and here too their countrymen rallied
to their aid. For a nominal fee, Will rented the loom of an
uncle, Andrew Hogan, and began weaving tablecloths,
which he peddled door-to-door. Margaret persuaded
Henry Phipps, a local cobbler, to parcel out shoe-binding
work to her. After a few weeks' search, Andrew got his
first job as a bobbin boy in a local textile mill whose
owner, Mr. Blackstock, another Scot, gave preferential
treatment to his countrymen. The job paid $1.20 a week.
"I have made millions since," Carnegie later claimed, "but
none of these gave me so much happiness as my first
week's earnings. I was now a helper of the family, a bread
winner." Although he found the work tedious and the
hours long, Carnegie stayed on until he found a better-
paying position in the bobbin factory of John Jay, yet
another Dunfermline expatriate.

Carnegie found his new duties—dipping bobbins into
an oil bath and firing the factory boiler—even more oner-
ous than his old ones. The oil smell nauseated him; the

boiler terrified him (ironic reactions in a lad who subsequently became an oil speculator and a railroad superintendent). But Carnegie persevered and occasionally merited a temporary clerical assignment in the factory office. These interludes provided not only welcome relief but also Carnegie's first exposure to accounting. While working for Jay, Andrew decided to learn double-entry bookkeeping and enrolled in a night school course across the river in Pittsburgh. The fact that he trudged through the dark winter nights across the bridge to Pittsburgh and back after a twelve-hour day amid bobbins and boilers, all at the age of fourteen, testifies to his determination to adapt to conditions in his new homeland, temporarily coming to terms with the factory system while struggling to lift himself through hard work and self-improvement. Across the Atlantic, Karl Marx, capitalism's fiercest nemesis, published *Communist Manifesto*, urging workers to unite to cast off their chains. Carnegie, embryonic capitalist *extraordinaire* had no intention of waiting for a revolution; he set out to make his own way within the system.

Will Carnegie, in contrast, showed little of his son's energy and adaptability. In Dunfermline, the steam mills had destroyed Will's world and undermined his place at the head of the family. "The change from hand-loom to steam-loom weaving was disastrous to our family," Andrew recalled. Because his father failed to recognize the impending revolution and could not deal with it when it came, Carnegie's mother, "that power which never failed in any emergency," stepped forward "to repair the family fortunes." Even before leaving Scotland, Margaret had replaced Will as principal wage earner and decision maker. It was she who decided to go to America, overcoming her husband's reluctance by insisting they must go for the sake of their two young sons. Their departure confirmed that Will had failed, not Margaret. She had performed her duties as wife and mother and, moreover, had annexed his role of provider. Although in the past Will had shown courage as a Radical agitator, independence in repudiating his family's Presbyterianism, and self-discipline in becoming a respected weaver, he left his homeland a beaten man.

The new homeland did nothing to restore Will's self-esteem. Politics offered no foothold; Americans already had the freedoms Will had fought for in England. Nor could he regain his role as provider. In Allegheny his attempts at weaving produced extremely meager returns with the result, as Carnegie later described it, that "as usual my mother came to the rescue . . . and in addition to attending to her household duties—for of course we had no servant—this wonderful woman, my mother, earned four dollars a week by binding shoes." When Andrew found his first job in Blackstock's mill, Margaret "bullyragged" Will away from the loom and into the same factory, where she hoped he could simultaneously watch out for his son and generate some income. Will, however, had no more stomach for such work in America than he had had in Scotland. He soon drifted back to his loom, his career as provider virtually finished.

For the rest of his life Will worked the loom sporadically, vainly attempting to preserve a shred of self-respect. He hawked his scanty products through the streets of Pittsburgh; when he found no buyers there, he rode steamboats to downriver towns on the Ohio to sell his wares. He became, in short, an itinerant peddler, the final confirmation of the shipwreck of his life.

Carnegie's past biographers have tended to dismiss his father simply as a weak man despite the courage and determination Will showed in his youth. Whether his deterioration resulted from weakness or perversity in clinging to obsolete ideas, his wife and elder son clearly thought him a failure, their love and respect gradually changing to shame and contempt. Though Carnegie's later reflections on that period of his life dealt with it in terms of his family alone, the Carnegies' struggles in fact typified those of countless families then and since. When technological change has fractured traditional roles by eliminating men's jobs, women, cheaper to hire and more adaptable, have gone to work. Declining male self-respect often followed, leading to a rise in alcoholism, domestic violence, and often, as with Will Carnegie, a fading will to live. The blight of spirit that the Carnegies experienced in Dunfermline and Pittsburgh has ever since beset families in dying industrial cities such as Lowell, Massachusetts, Youngstown, Ohio, and Wilkes-Barre, Pennsylvania, when the textile plants, steel mills, and coal mines closed.

Andrew Carnegie's feelings at the time of his father's death in 1855 surfaced in reflections in his *Autobiography:* "My father was one of the most lovable of men . . . not much of a man of the world, but a man all over for heaven"; faint praise indeed from one who abandoned religion as a boy, spent his Sundays ice-skating, reading, or riding horses, scoffed at the idea of heaven and at those who preached it, embraced the evolutionary dogmas of Herbert Spencer, and boasted of his own achievements as a "man of the world."

Andrew's remarks did his father a disservice. It was not so much that Will failed as a man of the world, but that his world had passed. He and his son belonged to different times, and nothing better symbolized their differences than the circumstances in which each left factory work. Will gave up in defeat and drifted back to the loom. Andrew stuck it out until he found a better job as messenger boy for the O'Reilly Telegraph Company. As the father faded into his past, the son climbed up on the wave of the future—the first electronic communications network, the "nervous system" of the new industrial world.

Carnegie's chance at O'Reilly's telegraph office resulted, as had so many earlier opportunities, from the cohesiveness of Pittsburgh's Scottish community; for the manager, David Brooks, also followed a policy of giving preference to Scottish immigrant boys. He and Carnegie's Uncle Hogan were frequent opponents at checkers. During one of their bouts, Brooks told the uncle that he needed another messenger boy and would gladly consider any candidate Hogan cared to nominate. Andrew leaped at the chance to escape the coal hole and oil vat. Margaret—never wavering in her belief that her son's present employment was beneath him—backed him up; together they put down the father's objections. Next morning Andrew presented himself to Brooks, declared his willingness to start work at once, and did so.

The swiftness with which Carnegie grasped this opportunity demonstrated his ability to recognize the potential of a new service or product and to seize an auspicious moment to associate himself with it. Time and again he manifested this acumen, shifting his talents from factory to telegraph, from telegraph to railroad, from railroad to iron and then steel, meanwhile investing his money in express companies, oil fields, sleeping cars, and telegraphs before he finally fused his energies and capital in Carnegie Steel. During the first twenty years of Carnegie's lifetime, the development of the steam locomotive and the telegraph brought more revolutionary change to transportation and communications than had occurred in all human history. The movement of people, goods, and information, hitherto shackled by the speed of wind and wave, the stride of man and beast, accelerated to the pace of the rushing locomotive and zinging electricity. This astonishing new technology transformed markets and business's ability to serve them. Riding the surging changes from one opportunity to another, Carnegie showed a talent indispensable to success: fastening not on ideas ahead of their time, for these inevitably fail, but rather grasping those whose time has come or better yet, those for which people have long waited. This gift never deserted him, and in time carried him, as he himself admitted, "beyond [his] wildest dreams."

The first step, however, came that spring day in 1849 when Carnegie, after less than a year of factory drudgery, escaped to a "paradise . . . heaven, as it seemed to me, with newspapers, pens, pencils, and sunshine." More important, he later recalled, "I felt that my foot was on the ladder and that I was bound to climb." The opportunity came, as he realized, from "Fortunatus" ("my Good Fairy found me in a cellar"); his own virtue lay in exploiting the chance.

When he joined the telegraph company in Pittsburgh in 1849, Carnegie positioned himself to observe closely a vital part of the transition in which the United States transferred much of its capital, manpower, and technology from the old agricultural world to the new industrial one. In the next decade, $800 million of capital built and equipped 22,000 miles of railroad. Merchants such as Anson Phelps, Benjamin Jones, James Laughlin, Edward Townsend, and others shifted their surplus capital from trade to manufacturing and influenced a few banks to follow. In this process Pittsburgh occupied a pivotal position. It sat astride a main east–west route at the confluence of the Monongahela and Allegheny rivers, which formed the Ohio. This junction tied the Pennsylvania Canal system to the commerce of the South and West by way of the Ohio, Mississippi, and Missouri river basins. Through the Ohio Canal the city also had access to the Great Lakes.

Pittsburgh also enjoyed excellent transportation routes to its own immediate hinterland. From the city the waterways radiated like the spokes of a wheel—the Ohio River to the west; the Conemaugh River east toward the iron mines and furnaces on the slopes of the Alleghenies; the Monongahela and Youghiogheny rivers south toward the coal deposits of Connellsville and West Virginia; the Allegheny and Clarion rivers north to iron and oil. As these natural resources were discovered and developed, the rivers funneled them to Pittsburgh. The city's location on the rivers thus facilitated its growth as an industrial center just as it had made Pittsburgh a major regional distribution center by tying it closely to the local farm economy. Pittsburgh's status as a major commercial center in the first decade of the early nineteenth century aided the city's subsequent growth as an iron manufacturing center—growth that had progressed far enough by 1849 to fill the sky with smoke and the river with slime. The land nearby held ample iron ore and abundant charcoal with which to smelt it, and was interlaced with creeks and rivers to transport raw materials to the furnaces and pig iron to Pittsburgh for further processing. The city offered a labor supply and facilities that serviced the workers' bodily and spiritual needs, thus relieving iron manufacturers of the responsibility of providing homes and services for the workers (a traditional problem for iron works situated in the hinterlands). It also facilitated recruitment of additional workers. "Come to Pittsburgh" proved a more effective siren song than "Come to a clearing in the middle of nowhere."

By 1849 Pittsburgh enjoyed a dual commercial and industrial economy, directed by an oligarchy of merchants and manufacturers. The two groups had worked together for some time; merchants supplied manufacturers' raw materials, sold their finished products, and were beginning to form capital alliances as well, largely by selling raw materials on credit and by making advances on products. Carnegie came to know many of these men as he plied the muddy streets delivering messages to them. Some—Edwin Stanton and Benjamin Jones, for example—achieved national prominence; others—Judge David McCandless, for one—later became business associates. Andrew prided himself on knowing the location of every business establishment in town, as well as the face of its proprietor. He began to accumulate an encyclopedic knowledge of local business, using his years at the telegraph office as a school of business practice.

Bright and observant, Carnegie soon knew as much about Pittsburgh's commercial affairs as anyone in town. He knew who sold how much of what to whom, when, at what price, and on what terms. He could hardly avoid learning who formed business alliances, overt and covert, and who were competitors. He knew who succeeded and who failed because information on the credit standing of firms and individuals passed through his hands every day.

Carnegie also saw the importance of telegraphic communication as a new component of business. The telegraph brought immediate communication between buyers and sellers. Negotiations over prices and terms; information on shipments, local and national market conditions, and credit ratings; and orders for goods and demands for services poured through the wires. Along with railroad passenger and express service, the availability of speedy communication brought revamped sales techniques. Commodity exchanges emerged to market farm crops. Drummers with suitcases of samples replaced peddlers selling from wagons. Salesmen telegraphed orders to the home office, which then shipped goods directly to the customer. In heavier industry, direct shipments from the factory often replaced cumbersome warehousing and consignment methods, reducing inventory and freeing capital for more productive use.

Andrew worked assiduously; he came early and stayed late. He swept out the office in the morning before it opened, then used his time to learn telegraphy. Rewards came apace: first, a raise from $2.50 to $3.00 a week, then a chance to work part-time as a telegraph operator. In 1851 the company promoted him to full-time operator. (The superintendent who approved the promotion was James D. Reid, born in Dunfermline.) Andrew wrote to his cousin George ("Dod") Lauder Jr. in Scotland, "I am past delivering messages now and have got to operating. I am to have four dollars a week and a good prospect of getting more."

Soon after becoming a full-time telegrapher, Carnegie determined to learn to take messages by ear, by "reading" the sound of the key rather than its printout. This art he quickly mastered, apparently one of the first telegraphers in America to do so. Within a year Andrew enjoyed a city-wide reputation as the city's best operator. He also dominated his fellow employees. In fact, he had recruited most of them, scrupulously perpetuating Scottish reciprocity by finding places for fellow Caledonians Robert Pitcairn, David McCargo, Henry Oliver, and Will Morland. After enlisting them, he kept them organized and disciplined. He persuaded them to pool all tips, thereby averting disputes over who carried what message. He kept them pushing the broom in the office and even cut off their credit in candy stores.

His ability to exact cooperation from his peers evidently rested on moral suasion, force of example, and understanding of human nature. As a boy in Scotland he had persuaded local urchins to feed and care for his growing brood of rabbits by allowing each volunteer to name a rabbit after himself. The trick worked; the rabbits got fed. (In fact, it worked so well that Carnegie repeated it on a much grander scale later on.) When he enrolled in accounting class, he talked friends Tom Miller and John Phipps into going along. He believed he could succeed and that they could also. To an astonishing degree events proved him right; Pitcairn and McCargo became railroad superintendents; Oliver and Tom Miller made fortunes both on their own and as partners in ventures with Carnegie; Morland became city solicitor; John Phipps died from a fall off a horse, but his younger brother Henry became Carnegie's lifelong partner and retired a multimillionaire.

Altogether the Carnegie of the telegraph office seems almost too good to be true, almost a caricature of a Horatio Alger figure. He seems the archetype of the worthy boy of a poor but honest family, working hard and studying at the same time, waiting confidently for his chance and then after getting it, still pushing forward to validate the trust and confidence of his superiors. Andrew went to school at night and read history and classics on weekends. Every step of the way—factory drudge, office boy, messenger, part-time telegrapher, full-time telegrapher—he pushed himself hard, mastered his duties, maximized the perceivable opportunities, and awaited with self-assurance the arrival of the next chance. His chance soon came, brought by his "good fairy," and he knew what to do when he got it.

In 1852 Tom Scott took over as superintendent of the Pennsylvania Railroad's western division. Impressed with Carnegie's work, Scott offered him a job as secretary and personal telegrapher; Carnegie accepted at once. His new job paid $35 a month but the raise was not the chief inducement; opportunity was. At his "old berth [he] must always have been an employee. The highest station [he] could attain was Manager of an office." Consequently, he had decided to accept any situation "which would be better for the future," even if it meant a temporary cut in salary. Attuned to the trends manifest in the flow of business information through the telegraph office, Carnegie had rightly perceived the railroads as the most dynamic industry in America, growing by leaps and bounds. Since his arrival in 1848, American railroads had nearly tripled their mileage, growing swiftly into America's "first big business," linking Pittsburgh to the Atlantic coast, pushing hard toward Cincinnati, St. Louis, and Chicago, with the ultimate goal of the Pacific coast. Among these booming railroads, the Pennsylvania was best of them all.

Joining the railroad at the age of seventeen, Carnegie had thus already exhibited most of the qualities that would carry him to wealth and power. In addition to working so hard and believing in his own destiny, he had enough charisma to persuade others to follow him. He made the right friends; he admired strength and despised weakness. Although loyal, kind, and independent in his dealings with most people, he showed streaks of guile and obsequiousness now and again. Physically durable (an asset often underrated as a component of success) and mentally acute, he had a retentive memory and an uncanny instinct for opportunity. The years in the telegraph office put these qualities through a basic training in business, adding acquired techniques to inherent talent. The railroad presented an unprecedented challenge; he assaulted it with the same restless ambition he had always shown.

And what made Andy run? Why did he feel that "whatever I engage in I must push inordinately"? Certain obvious factors suggest themselves. He was a small boy and a short man (five-feet-three-inches full grown at a time when the average American male stood five-feet-seven). His father was a weak parent and his mother a strong one. Andrew felt driven to prove his manhood and he had to compete with his brother for his mother's love. Success in the business world soothed his self-doubts and the guilt feelings that afflicted many immigrants.

Emigration usually was an admission of an inability to cope with life at home. No matter how severe the vicissitudes that prompted their departure, expatriates often felt that their own shortcomings had played a major part. As a result, many immigrants felt driven to prove themselves in their new country, to show the folks at home that having failed once they could succeed on the second try. Margaret and Andrew Carnegie both dreamed of the day when they could return in triumph to Dunfermline. The most splendid occasion—perhaps the most satisfying moment of Margaret Carnegie's life—came in 1881 when Carnegie presented his birthplace with a new library. The city held a commemorative parade, eight thousand marchers strong, with banners reading "Welcome Carnegie, Generous Son." Mother and son brought up the rear of the procession, riding in a palatial coach-and-four, passing in triumph through the town they had once fled in poverty.

During his first few years in the United States, Carnegie's letters home bristled with vindication of the family's move. Each advance in salary and every promotion provided an occasion for a sermon (usually directed to Cousin Dod Lauder) on the virtues of the new country. "We have all of your good traits," Carnegie wrote, "and few of your bad ones. . . . We go ahead. I would have been a poor weaver all my days, but here, I can surely do something better . . . if I don't it will be my own fault, for anyone can get along in this country." At Uncle Lauder's prompting, he and his cousin carried on an epistolary debate on the relative merits of the two countries' political systems. Carnegie leaped nimbly over such faults as slavery and dwelt at length on what he saw as the republic's merits: its free press, small military and police forces, cheap postal service, upright politicians, freedom from stultifying traditions, willingness to innovate.

But greatest of all its virtues was the democratic political process and the economic benefits derived from it: "We now possess what the working classes of Your Country look forward to as constituting their political millennium. We have the charter which you have been fighting for for years as the panacea for all Britain's woes, the bulwark of the liberties of the people." Possession of the charter, Carnegie thought, made America's economic dominance inevitable: "The best proof of the superiority of our system is seen in the general prosperity." The national treasury held a surplus; the public debt was paid as it matured; the western lands were filling up; 13,000 miles of railroad and 21,000 miles of telegraph had been built with thousands more on the way; pauperism rarely occurred. These benefits derived from the government that existed by the consent of the governed. What else could explain

> . . . the contrast between the U States and the Canadas? They were settled by the same people, at the same time, under the same government—and look at the difference! Where are her Railroads, Telegraphs and Canals? her commercial marine and her unrivalled steamships? her fast clippers or her potent Press? We have given to the world a Washington, a Franklin, a Fulton, a Morse—what has Canada ever produced?

All his life Carnegie adhered to this theme of the interdependence between political equality and economic superiority. This equation served Carnegie as a two-edged sword: with one side he attacked other countries' systems as inferior; with the other he defended American institutions against criticism. In the United States most things were right; those which were not would improve or disappear because the system was self-correcting. This handy credo excused all kinds of economic abuses and justified opposition to economic reforms either by government intervention or by labor agitation. If the business world reformed, then, Carnegie argued, it would inevitably come as a consequence of the political system. Carnegie clung to this belief despite demonstrations of extensive political corruption and evidence of widespread economic abuse, including some perpetrated by Carnegie himself.

Joseph Wall, Carnegie's most exhaustive biographer, explains Carnegie's attitudes more as a result of "arrested development" than of hypocrisy. Carnegie left Scotland before systematic doctrines of economic reform such as socialism came into public consciousness. He espoused Scottish Radicalism, largely expressed in opposition to the Corn Laws (a tariff on imported grain), support of the Charter, and "death to privilege" (abolition of hereditary aristocracies). Americans had long since attained these goals, and Carnegie "looked no further into the meaning of liberalism." Undoubtedly this accounted for Carnegie's rationale. His obstinate adherence to it in the face of massive contradictions—he was, after all, not unobservant, stupid, unfeeling, nor incapable of changing—bespoke a deeper emotion, rooted in a personal commitment. Also, he defended the American system so vigorously because its triumph was his own triumph; its virtues were his virtues; and its success justified his wealth and the ways he acquired it. Attacks on the system attacked him. If the system were virtuous, then Carnegie was a Horatio Alger hero personified; if the system were evil, then he had traded his Scottish birthright for a mess of American pottage and left his fellow Scots to fight for the Charter while he himself focused on making himself rich.

But even with all these things said, the ultimate source of Carnegie's consuming ambition remains elusive. Plenty of undersized Scottish immigrant boys had parents who reversed roles, sibling jealousies, and self-doubts without evincing Andrew Carnegie's relentless yearning for power.

Indeed, Andrew had one such at his elbow, his own brother Tom, who, Andrew said, "was born tired." Tom bobbed reluctantly along in his brother's wake, yearning for peace and quiet, and eventually opted for a bibulous escape. Similar circumstances thus forged contrasting personalities within the same family.

Ultimately human behavior results from the ways in which individuals accommodate themselves to the contradictions and ambiguities within themselves and their society. Most of these conflicts defy resolution; they can only be rationalized. Andrew Carnegie had a personal set of paradoxes. The best his biographers can do is to designate the pressures and document the response. The precise motivation always remains something of a mystery, and therein lies both the fascination and frustration of history. In himself Carnegie knew kindness and cruelty, vanity and shame, generosity and greed, doubt and confidence. Somehow this added up to optimism about himself and his new country. In the new environment he met bitter competition and kindly helpers, noxious squalor and opulent wealth, corrupted politics and selfless charity. This constituted a system he determined to master, and strive he did, largely oblivious to events outside his self-absorbed orbit.

As Carnegie moved from telegraph to railroad office in 1852, his adopted country lurched toward the Civil War that would tear it apart. That same year, Harriet Beecher Stowe's *Uncle Tom's Cabin,* the most provocative American anti-slavery work ever published appeared; Henry Clay and Daniel Webster, the country's greatest surviving statesmen, died; the Compromise of 1850, designed to calm the slavery crisis had achieved the reverse. If any of these menacing events concerned Carnegie, he left no hint of it in his memoirs, which focus on the event that mattered to him, his new appointment as Tom Scott's fair-haired boy. He left O'Reilly's telegraph office with his apprenticeship far advanced. He approached his new job on the railroad thinking "Death or Westminster Abbey." He had a long life ahead.

Thomas A. Scott

III

The Apprentice Manager

Carnegie's twelve years' experience on the Pennsylvania Railroad shaped his subsequent career. On the railroad he assimilated the managerial skills, grasped the economic principles, and cemented the personal relationships that enabled him to become successively manager, capitalist, and entrepreneur. His most spectacular achievement—building Carnegie Steel into the world's largest steel producer—rested primarily on his successful transfer of the railroads' managerial methods to the manufacturing sector of the economy. The first industrialist to effect this adaptation, he made his own company so efficient that his competitors had to emulate or eliminate him. Carnegie thus played a critical role in the genesis of the American system of manufacturing that built the United States into the world's leading industrial power by 1900.

The railroads developed modern bureaucratic structures because they had no choice. Their size and complexity precluded the use of traditional methods of finance and management. They had to develop quickly a new organization that would result in profitable operation or else go bankrupt. The Pennsylvania Railroad achieved this goal sooner and more effectively than any other railroad in the world. It had essentially completed its organization (ultimately copied by many railroads in America and Britain) by 1865 when Carnegie left its employ. He had witnessed the creation of the structure and policy, and he had played an influential role as superintendent of the western division during unprecedented growth in traffic. To appreciate fully the relation between Carnegie's successful railroad experience and his later achievements first requires considering the problems the railroads faced and how they resolved them.

Railroads differed from preceding business institutions in sheer size. Before the first railroads appeared in the 1830s, the largest American industrial units were the textile mills of New England. Even the biggest of these could be explored, nook and cranny, in an afternoon's leisurely stroll. On the other hand, the facilities of a very small railroad, say thirty or forty miles of route, with such requisite ancillaries as stations, warehouses, repair shops, offices, and roundhouses, took days to tour on foot. Moreover, unlike the textile mill with its five or six working floors lined with machines, only a fraction of the railroad's operations could be seen at one time by a given observer.

Because of their size, construction of railroads demanded massive amounts of capital, and the demands increased as the roads expanded. By 1850 sixteen American railroads operated two hundred and fifty or more miles of line; two of them capitalized at more than $10 million. By 1859 ten had grown as large, and half of these exceeded $20 million in outlay. In order to assemble such large amounts of money, the railroads had to tap the savings of the public, and had to enlist the support of major investors both in the United States and in Europe. Railroad promoters much preferred to raise capital by selling stock, which entailed surrendering a measure of corporate sovereignty but involved no borrowing and hence no annual interest bill to pay. Investors, on the other hand, often preferred bonds, which constituted a mortgage on the company's assets and which paid a stipulated annual rate of interest. Some railroads had to pay painfully high interest rates in order to attract financial support. These payments saddled the firm with "fixed costs"; that is, costs that did not vary with the volume of business and indeed had to be paid even if the firm had no income at all.

In the long run, most American railroads were capitalized more by bonds than by stock. Some instances reached extremes: $17 million of the Illinois Central's first $18 million came from bonds; the Erie financed its construction costs with $6 million from stock sales and a $21 million bonded debt. By 1855 American railroads operated over 18,000 route miles and had a $300 million bonded debt; in 1867, 39,000 miles and $417 million. Meeting the fixed costs of such financing was one of the unprecedented problems railroad managers faced. Throughout the nineteenth century more than 20 percent of the railroads' gross operating earnings went to pay interest on funded debts.

Meeting the annual interest bill was just one of the tricks that railroad managers had to learn. They also had to find ways to run the trains, maintain the track and rolling stock, price their services, and collect the charges— all at a profit. As business expanded, these tasks grew in complexity. Receipts rose from $40 million in 1851 to $84 million in 1855, to $130 million in 1860, and to $334 million in 1867. Many railroads soon had to run passenger and freight trains in both directions around the clock to meet the demand, operations that required well-coordinated communications and discipline to avoid wrecks.

The system of train control which American railroads developed accomplished a managerial revolution that brought more change in business decision making and operational methods in twenty-five years than had occurred in the preceding five centuries. Before the railroad most business decisions depended on experience, instinct, and information, often little better than guesswork. Orders passed from proprietors, overseers, or foremen to workers, who carried them out with little sense of urgency. Tobacco and cotton farmers, in contrast, simply grew all they could and trusted to good luck in the market. Their labor forces frequently fluctuated in size, skill, and disposition to work. Textile mills used more complex methods of planning and control but retained many pre-industrial operations. For example, they planned type, quantity, and color of cloth from the estimates of the commission merchants who marketed the goods. Merchants based their own recommendations on experiential guesswork. They often guessed wrong, causing unsold goods or unsatisfied demands. But if they guessed right, the mill made enough money to compensate for bad years. The treasurer passed production orders to floor foremen. Just as on the plantations, absent, lazy, incompetent, or stupid hands might decrease production slightly, but on the whole, individual deviations had little effect on the total operation. If an employee disobeyed orders, only that output was lost; no serious damage was done.

No such casual arrangements could obtain on the railroads. Using the telegraph, train dispatchers controlled movements on the basis of fresh, complete information. Safe, prompt train movement required highly disciplined workers. Because all movements were tightly interlocked, one employee could bring everything to a standstill; unreliable, incompetent, or insubordinate workers had to go. The railroad also required literate, intelligent employees because it operated by a system of written rules and orders, and because stupidity could cause wrecks, damage property, and kill people.

Collecting railroad revenues presented crucial and unprecedented problems of management. Previously, most businesses had derived their income from a relatively small number of large sales. Textile mills and iron manufacturers sold their entire output through one or two commission merchants, often under an exclusive contract. They rarely settled accounts more often than once a month. Consequently, an entire year's output might result in less than two or three dozen payments to the manufacturer and finally, these payments rarely involved cash. Merchants paid with notes or other commercial paper, which functioned then much as checks do now.

In sharp contrast, the railroads collected their million-dollar revenues in hundreds of thousands of individual transactions, the great majority of them in cash: quite literally a nickel and dime business. Most of this cash went first into the hands of conductors and station agents. A passenger train conductor often made more collections in an hour than a textile mill did in a year. To ensure that this river of coin flowed into the company's treasury, not into the employees' pockets, required a system of numbered tickets and freight waybills, unique conductors' punches (no two alike and all registered), and station accounts, all supervised by a central office.

Finally, the complexity of railroad equipment demanded coordination of various specialized skills. Railroads employed boilermakers, pipe fitters, sheet-metal workers, carpenters, car repairmen, track inspectors and mechanics, telegraph and signal maintenance men. The work of these experts required precise coordination to keep them out of each other's way and to cause a minimum of delay to traffic.

Only one organization, the military, had experience moving large quantities of men and material across long distances. The railroads adapted the military's line and staff organization, often using military nomenclature—division, semaphore, and court-martial. Sometimes they recruited as managers professional soldiers such as Isaac Trimble, superintendent of the Philadelphia, Wilmington, and Baltimore, and George McClellan, president of the Ohio and Mississippi. These men and others like them perfected the first modern bureaucracies for management, capable of controlling complex, round-the-clock operations at places distant from headquarters and coordinated with telegraphic speed.

The pioneer architect of this system of management, Daniel McCallum, general superintendent of the Erie in the 1850s, advocated discipline first and foremost: all levels of management had to enforce the rules: "All that is required to render the efforts of railroad companies in every respect equal to that of individuals, is a rigid system of personal accountability through every grade of service." Under McCallum's system the Book of Rules and the Employees' Timetable spelled out each employee's responsibilities and authority. Failure to perform according to standard furnished grounds for suspension, demotion, or dismissal.

With such methods, bureaucratic management transformed the casual workforce of the old pre-industrial world into a disciplined industrial army of unprecedented size. In the 1850s most cotton plantations had fewer than a hundred workers, and the largest nonrailroad employer, the Pepperell Mills at Biddeford, Maine, had eight hundred workers. At the same time, the Pennsylvania and the Erie railroads each employed more than four thousand people and shaped them into disciplined workforces.

Operating such large institutions presented great difficulties; doing so at a profit proved an even greater challenge. The railroads' operating expenses greatly surpassed those of other large industrial units. Pepperell Mills' annual costs exceeded $300 thousand only once in the 1850s. In 1855 the Erie had expenses of $2.8 million; the Pennsylvania's were $2.1 million and reached $5.4 million by 1862. These variable operating expenses, combined with the fixed costs of debt retirement, interest payments, and taxes, demanded a substantial and continuing cash flow. Moreover, just to break even by balancing operating costs against operating revenues would not suffice—something had to remain to pay interest on the debt. Fixed costs thus imposed the ultimatum of either operating at a profit or facing bankruptcy. In addition, although the railroad had no legal obligation to pay dividends to stockholders, it more or less had to, because otherwise stockholders would refuse to raise additional capital for future expansion or improvements.

For railroad managers, the need to maintain a cash flow and have a net income often dictated conflicting policies. In the 1850s and 1860s, the usual way to generate revenue was to cut prices. If, however, the price fell below cost, then increased business was disastrous, for losses mounted rapidly. The elusive equipoise between prices and costs depended, in the words of Daniel McCallum of the Erie, on "the minimum amount of service consistent with the largest net revenue . . . which must mainly depend upon data received from the actual expenses and earnings of each train."

In brief, by the mid-1850s, railroad managers realized that prices must be based on actual costs, not left merely to market forces. A service that used the least possible amount of equipment must be provided. Cars should be kept fully loaded, and each train should carry as many cars as the engine could haul. This was the formula for profitable operation of a capital-intensive business: learn the costs and reduce them as much as possible; then lower prices to lure a greater volume of business. Reduced prices then increase profits by keeping the capital assets employed near capacity. If costs, however, are not accurately known, reduced prices might only pile up losses. If the volume taxes capacity, then concentrate on efficiency: run the trains faster, turn the equipment more quickly. Profitability in the long run hinges on the management's ability to maximize traffic flow and minimize unit cost. By trial and error the railroads learned, often painfully, the lessons of running a capital-intensive business, financed with OPM ("other people's money") that burdened them with fixed costs and demanded strict accounting of all income and expenditures. In the years since, technology has changed dramatically, but the principles for managing it profitably remain essentially the same as those developed by American railroads in the 1850s.

The Pennsylvania certainly confronted all the problems typical of a large and expanding railroad. Its original terminals, Philadelphia and Pittsburgh, lay almost 300 miles apart. From its inception it expanded aggressively east and west, so that in thirty years it operated 3,500 miles of main track, owned hundreds of locomotives and thousands of cars, and had 30,000 employees and a capital investment of $61 million. By 1865 it was the largest private business firm in the world in revenues, employees, and value of physical assets.

Furthermore, the Pennsylvania was a mountain railroad—the largest mountain railroad in the world. Operating such a line presented additional problems. More trains were required to move the same volume of traffic, since each train had to be shorter than on level track. Operating many short trains required more track space than a few long ones. Consequently, mountain railroading involved heavy capital investment in equipment and high operating costs for fuel, train crews' wages, maintenance of engines, cars, and tracks, and snow clearance in winter.

The Pennsylvania Railroad's management sorted out its labyrinth of financial and operating problems so effectively that it became known as "the standard railroad of the world." The principal architects of the bureaucratic structure making that achievement possible were J. Edgar Thomson, the railroad's first president, and Tom Scott, superintendent of its western division. By working in close association with these men, Carnegie absorbed the fundamentals of sound management. Indeed, the process of developing a modern system of train control first brought Carnegie and Scott together.

Scott hired Carnegie as his personal telegrapher to assist him in dispatching trains over the western division's mountainous main line. Although Scott originally intended to use the O'Reilly company's facilities, he soon decided that he needed a permanent staff of railroad telegraphers and a telegraph line exclusively for the railroad. The latter he got from Thomson, the former he turned over to Carnegie, who promptly lured his friends David McCargo and Robert Pitcairn from the telegraph company. (Both went on to become superintendents.) Establishing the railroad's telegraph service marked the first joint effort by the triumvirate of Thomson, Scott, and Carnegie.

Carnegie worked hard to maximize his opportunity by becoming Scott's right-hand man. Meeting the railroad's customers, discussing their needs for service, observing the kinds of shipments made and received, Carnegie added to his growing knowledge of commerce and the men who controlled it. Dealing with the railroad's laborers brought him into contact with a hard-bitten class of people he had seldom encountered before. Aided by Scott's example, he learned how to jolly this motley crew into working hard and loyally, a skill that served him well in years to come.

He also mastered the intricacies of controlling the division's operations. One morning a derailment brought all traffic to a standstill. Carnegie arrived at the office to find that Scott had not yet appeared. Sizing up the situation, he recognized that fate had placed another opportunity in his path. He promptly sent messages that got the traffic moving, signing them T. A. S. because only the superintendent had the authority to issue train orders. Thereafter, train movements became the responsibility of full-time dispatchers, to whom superintendents delegated their authority, thus institutionalizing Carnegie's extemporaneous solution. His willingness to take charge showed his customary self-reliance; it also demonstrated that he had learned railroad operations thoroughly. In order to set a mass of trains in motion, Carnegie had to have a mental blueprint of one hundred miles of track, correct in every detail, including the length and location of passing sidings; the location, order, and distance between stations; the position of fuel supplies and water tanks for locomotives. The fact that, as Carnegie described it, "all was right" indicated that in less than a year he had achieved a complete familiarity with the most sophisticated railroad operation in America.

Scott had high regard for Carnegie's abilities. In 1855, when Carnegie was twenty years old and had served on the railroad two years, Scott left town on a ten-day trip, leaving Carnegie in charge of the division. A "pretty bold" move on Scott's part, as Carnegie recalled it, but it gave him "the coveted opportunity of my life." During the superintendent's absence Carnegie had only one serious problem. His handling of it foreshadowed a later situation when he felt his employees were misusing him:

> . . . everything went well . . . with the exception of one accident caused by the inexcusable negligence of a ballast train crew. . . . That this accident should occur was gall and wormwood to me. Determined to fill all the duties of the station I held a court martial . . . dismissed peremptorily the chief offender, and suspended two others for their share in the catastrophe.

Scott considered the sentences excessive but backed up his subordinate.

While Carnegie and Scott were developing effective methods of operation, Thomson perfected an accounting system. In 1854 he made giving accounts a regular duty for officials in every department. These accounts recorded all revenues and expenditures in minute detail. As a stockholders' committee reported: "A charge or entry of a day's labor, of the purchase of a keg of nails, or the largest order goes through such a system of checks and audits as to make fraud almost an impossibility."

In addition to income and expense accounts, detailed statistics chronicled train mileage, freight tonnage, and the number of passengers, delays, and breakdowns. All data, first collected in the smallest administrative unit, were then aggregated at the divisional level, with records kept for each locomotive on the system twenty-four hours a day showing time in service, time out of service with steam up, time out of service with firebox cold, time out of service for repairs, and so on and on—a statistician's paradise.

These statistics yielded a variety of performance indices. The most important data revealed which services profited and which lost, which division operated efficiently and which did not. The reports also pinpointed specific sources of success and failure and guided managers' decisions on such questions as raising or lowering rates, increasing or curtailing service, making repairs or postponing them.

The task of translating the statistical returns into management policy fell to Scott. In 1855 Thomson appointed him general superintendent, and he and Carnegie moved to Altoona, where they remained until 1859. To keep profits up, Scott minimized costs per ton-mile by maximizing train loads. Bigger cars, bigger locomotives, longer trains, minimal delays drove the ton-mile costs down. Rates were set at any level above cost that would keep cars and trains loaded to capacity. Capital investments were judged on their potential for reducing unit costs or adding to traffic volume. To reduce unit costs, the Pennsylvania expanded its Altoona shops for the manufacture of heavy cars and engines, laid double tracks in densely trafficked sections to reduce delays, and relocated the main line over the mountains to ease grade and curvature. To increase traffic volume, the Pennsylvania expanded aggressively east and west into New York and Chicago. In short, the Pennsylvania under Thomson and Scott concentrated capital investment on projects that began paying for themselves at once by reducing unit costs or increasing unit revenue more than they added to capital costs.

Scott also used cost data in promoting or discharging supervisors. He judged one man against another, and measured each man against his own previous performance. Supervisors continually had to find ways to reduce costs. Officials often received a warning along with new appointments: find a saving or get a new job.

This policy, like so many others, the Pennsylvania drafted from Daniel McCallum. Use of comparative cost data, McCallum argued in 1856,

> . . . will show the officers who conduct their business with the greatest economy, and will indicate, in a manner not to be mis-

taken, the relative ability and fitness of each for the position he occupies. . . . It will be valuable in pointing out the particulars of excess in the cost of management of one division over another [and] will direct attention to those matters in which sufficient economy is not practiced.

The effect of all this on the officers themselves would be to "excite an honorable spirit of emulation to excel."

Scott installed this system of meritocracy, which lasted through the nineteenth century. By 1864 it had been codified in the "Book of Rules": "Employees of every grade, will be considered in line of promotion, dependent . . . upon qualifications, and capacity for assuming increased responsibility." Contemporary observers frequently cited the policy as a major reason for the Pennsylvania's success. The *Railroad Gazette,* for example, commented in 1882 on "the resistance to outside influences which would place men in office on the ground of [considerations] other than proved merit." "We do thoroughly believe," it added, "that merit and training are the most potent of all influences in giving positions of every kind upon the road."

The results that the Pennsylvania Railroad achieved with its system of management formed a recurring theme in the industry literature in America and England in the second half of the nineteenth century. Although a ferocious critic of railroads in general, Charles Francis Adams called the Pennsylvania "that superb organization, every detail of whose wonderful system is a fit subject for study to all interested in the operation of railroads." Many American lines such as the Burlington openly copied its methods and structures. Even British railroad officers toured it regularly and used its statistics as a yardstick to measure their own companies' performance.

This efficient organization obviously had little margin of tolerance for incompetent executives, so when Scott became vice-president of the Pennsylvania in 1859 and appointed Carnegie superintendent of the western division, he demonstrated his faith in Carnegie's competence. After all, Scott was not simply filling a political sinecure; he was filling the most demanding railroad division superintendency in America.

The job demanded twenty-four-hour attention. As Carnegie described it, "The superintendent of a division in those days was expected to run trains by telegraph at night, to go and remove all wrecks, and indeed to do everything. At one time for eight days I was constantly upon the line, day and night, at one obstruction or the other." He gloried in it. He had dreamed of someday being in Scott's place, signing documents with his own name. When Scott offered him the appointment, Carnegie said:

> I was only twenty-four years old, but my model then was Lord John Russell of whom it was said he would take command of the Channel Fleet tomorrow.

To Scott's remarks about salary, Carnegie expostulated that he cared nothing about salary: "I want the position. It is glory enough to go back to the Pittsburgh Division in your former place." He was to have the power and he reveled in the symbol of it, "I was to have a department to myself, and instead of signing 'T. A. S.' orders between Pittsburgh and Altoona would now be signed 'A. C.'"

Carnegie performed well as superintendent, for he thoroughly understood the cost–volume–velocity doctrines, the operating strategies that put them into practice, and the complex statistical analyses that had produced them. He proved himself a daring innovator. He cleared wrecks by burning the cars that blocked the line, or by laying new tracks around them. On his own authority he appointed the first night train dispatchers to facilitate twenty-four-hour movements, and persuaded his superiors to keep all telegraph stations open around the clock. He forwarded a stream of proposals for improvements in service and cost cutting to headquarters, always supporting them with statistical analyses. He proposed, for example, that the entire main line between Altoona and Pittsburgh be double-tracked to reduce train delays, and that train crews' hours of service be lengthened from ten to thirteen to eliminate a crew change between the two cities. Carnegie also used equipment to the maximum extent possible. In 1861 he cut Pittsburgh commuter fares to meet competition and keep trains full. On another occasion he beat down costs below the competitors' because he eliminated "the hidden ebbs and flows of trade" by holding back shipments of the company's own materials such as coal and lumber until "movement [was] light." Then such traffic "carried at company convenience [was] sufficient to keep the equipment active."

The years 1859–1865, during which Carnegie served as superintendent, proved crucial in the Pennsylvania Railroad's development. Traffic quadrupled; the road expanded from 367 to 856 miles; and fixed costs rose as the funded debt grew to finance capital improvements. Increasing efficiency enabled management to maintain profits and dividends throughout this period of growth. (In fact, the Pennsylvania paid dividends to its stockholders every year of its existence until the last, 1967.) Ton-mile costs fell as tons moved per engine mile rose. Carnegie succeeded so well in his post that Thomson offered him a promotion to general superintendent in 1865. He declined, because he had decided to leave the railroad, but Thomson's offer testified to Carnegie's mastery of the complex responsibilities.

By the time Carnegie resigned his railroad position he had matured as a man and as a manager. He came to the

Pennsylvania a poor, ambitious messenger boy and left it a polished executive. Shifting from the telegraph company to the railroad furthered his knowledge of local and national business and continued his education in the ways of the industrial world. In his father's world the power of a single hand had moved only the loom; in Andrew's, a man's hand on a throttle or his finger on a telegraph key set hundreds of passengers and tons of freight in motion. In Will's world, business decisions had been made from simple criteria: a man worked hard as long as there was work to do, and hoped for the best; in good times and bad he relied on tradition, experience, and the advice of colleagues and relatives. In Andrew's domain, decisions depended on information gathered from impersonal statistics, and were carried out by a bureaucratic staff of men who often were complete strangers.

Between 1852 and 1865, while Carnegie honed his business skills to a fine, enduring edge, the United States grappled with the problems of a nation half-slave and half-free until, through force of arms, it established the indissolubility of the Federal Union and abolished the horrific national blemish of slavery. Tom Scott's call in April 1862 for Carnegie's help in setting up a system to dispatch Union Army trains in northern Virginia exposed Carnegie to the horror of trains laden with bleeding wounded returning from the battlefield of Bull Run. This brief experience (he returned to Pittsburgh in September 1862) with war filled him with a lifelong loathing of it. When drafted in 1864, he purchased a substitute, as the law then allowed. He justified this as he had justified his retreat to Pittsburgh: on the grounds that he best served the war effort by running the Pennsylvania Railroad's western division.

When Carnegie left the railroad on March 28, 1865, Grant's army had at last reached Richmond, and the

Confederacy had only days to live. For his part, Carnegie had completed his apprenticeship. He had learned his art. No further challenge remained in working for others. "A man must necessarily occupy a narrow field," he wrote, "who is at the beck and call of others." He had "determined to make a fortune." In 1865 he resigned. He never spent another day on a payroll.

The Eads Bridge in St. Louis, Missouri, built by the Keystone Bridge Company

I V

The Apprentice Financier

Carnegie's rise from bobbin boy to railroad superintendent makes a scenario that Horatio Alger himself might
have scripted. Carnegie the executive, like Ragged Dick
and Mark the Match Boy, rises not from rags to riches, but
rather from rags ($1.20 a week) to respectability ($2,400
a year). Here the similarity ends, however, for Carnegie,
unlike Alger's single-minded stalwarts, diversified his energies. In 1856 while still on the railroad he began his career
as a capitalist, and by 1863, investments, not salary, had
made him rich. After leaving the Pennsylvania Railroad he
never again worked hard in the classic sense. He still
applied himself energetically to his various responsibilities,
but he punctuated his labors with frequent and extended
vacations, world tours, and sabbaticals in Scotland.

Tom Scott introduced Carnegie to the wonders of capital investment, just as he had schooled him in the art of
management, and Carnegie proved as apt a pupil in the
one as in the other. In 1856 Scott persuaded him to buy ten
shares of Adams Express Company stock for $600, lend-
ing him the money. In the process he made himself an early
entrant in the ultimately vast American securities market.

In the 1850s, few firms other than railroads raised capital through sale of shares to the public; most of those that did, like Adams Express, functioned as railroad satellites. Untutored in the secrets of capitalism and wary of debt, Carnegie took the plunge because his hero told him to: "I had not fifty dollars saved for investment, but I was not going to miss the chance of becoming financially connected with my leader and great man."

Scott provided Carnegie with the strong father figure he had never had. They had much in common: a poverty-stricken childhood lacking in paternal leadership, a restless drive to succeed, an ability to master detail, a charismatic personality, and a determination to acquire through self-education the culture and urbanity that circumstances had denied them. In this case Andrew's fealty to Scott paid quick dividends in the form of a $10 check from Adams Express.

This first dividend check opened a new world. As Carnegie recalled in his *Autobiography*, "I shall remember that check for as long as I live. . . . It gave me the first penny of revenue from capital—something that I had not worked for with the sweat of my brow. 'Eureka,' I cried, 'Here's the goose that lays the golden eggs.'" Making money by a method other than toiling lay quite outside the experience of Carnegie and his Allegheny companions. When they had their weekly get-together on Sunday afternoon (Carnegie, John Phipps, Bob Pitcairn, David McCargo, Tom Miller—all immigrants or sons of immigrants), Andy proudly exhibited his check: "The effect produced upon my companions was overwhelming. None of them had imagined such an investment possible."

From this modest beginning Carnegie built a fortune. In 1863 his ventures provided an income of $45,460; to a friend who asked how he was, Carnegie replied, "I'm rich; I'm rich." In 1868 he was even richer; he owned securities and partnership shares worth $400,000 that paid him $56,110 a year. (He originally invested only $817, all of it borrowed.) Thus by the age of twenty-eight, Carnegie had made not one but two careers in the world of business and industry. In the first he had mastered the new art of managing a complex, multi-unit industrial enterprise. In the second he had penetrated the mysteries of capitalism, applying his knowledge with a skill that eventually vanquished a formidable array of business rivals, including Cornelius Vanderbilt, John Murray Forbes, Jay Gould, John D. Rockefeller, and J. P. Morgan.

The successful capitalist views money as something to use to make more money, not as something to spend; its value depends on what it will earn, not on what it will buy. One has to overthrow the consumer's mentality and replace it with the accumulator's. The $600 Carnegie borrowed to buy the Adams Express stock did more to make him rich than the $550 the family borrowed to buy their house; by 1863 the stock paid $1,440 a year in dividends. But buying the house came from a natural impulse; buying the stock did not. Realizing that the $10 dividend check represented money earned without working, Carnegie took his first step toward the investor's mentality. He also learned the important corollary that it made no difference whose money was invested. If the return exceeded the cost, it made sense to invest borrowed money. The Adams investment, for example, paid dividends ten times the interest on the loan in the first year that Carnegie held it.

Once entrenched, the investor's mentality exerted a constant pressure to find profitable investments. Since money was not something to spend, the capitalist had no desire to retrieve the principal of his investment as long as the return remained adequate. (Thus while the property owner rejoices at the burning of a mortgage, the banker busily searches for a new borrower.) Such pressure to find profitable investments had enormous economic leverage for it meant that entrepreneurs could assemble huge amounts of capital as long as investors foresaw adequate returns. The spectacular economic growth of the United States stemmed in major part from the fact that from its colonial beginnings, America benefited from practitioners of investment on both sides of the Atlantic. In fact, the very existence of the American colonies depended on private investors seeking profits from New World enterprises. By the time Andrew Carnegie learned the investor's art, it, like the American Dream of mobility, had hardened into a tradition two centuries old.

Carnegie learned, as had generations of investors before him, that raising capital often involved little actual money because anything that could generate an income—buildings, land, machinery, raw materials—could serve as well as cash. These things were usually obtained on credit in nineteenth-century America. Suppliers accepted either interest-bearing notes, bonds, or—if they had enough faith—stock in the new firm. The firm preferred the last, of course, for it involved no debts. Consequently, firms often offered three, four, five, or even ten dollars in stock for every dollar's worth of material or services. In this way, suppliers and contractors became investors. Railroads commonly used this method, often meeting half their construction costs by paying contractors, locomotive and car builders, and rail mills with their securities. Such deals involved considerable risk because bankruptcy meant total loss to stockholders and serious reverses for note- and bond-holders. On the other hand, stocks could bring enormous rewards. If the enterprise prospered and met its payments, the market value of its securities rose, multiplying the value of the investment.

The successful capitalist could accurately estimate a firm's potential profits. The investors who survived knew how to take "risks" in such a way that they ran no actual risk at all. They profited through interest and dividends and through the increased value of their holdings, which multiplied as the national economy grew. Under Tom

Scott's tutelage Carnegie learned to collect interest rather than pay it, and he became a shrewd judge of the growth potential of investment opportunities. In time the pupil outstripped his master, for Scott, a plunger, did not limit his risks, and eventually went under. Carnegie, on the other hand, remained the canny Scotsman. "I am sure," he said, "that any competent judge would be surprised how little I ever risked. . . . When I did big things some large corporation was behind me and [was] the responsible party. My supply of Scotch caution [was] never small."

Caution played an integral part in Carnegie's invest-ments; so far as possible he minimized risks, largely restricting himself to fields in which he had made himself an expert. His undertook his few ventures into unknown areas in conjunction with knowledgeable friends. The Adams Express investment had taught him the value of inside information; thereafter he primarily invested in firms that counted on the Pennsylvania Railroad for a large share of their business. Since Carnegie carefully allied himself with Thomson and Scott, the company's president and vice-president, the expectations of profitable sales invariably materialized.

The first of Carnegie's railroad-supported investments, the Woodruff Sleeping Car Company venture, illustrates the Carnegie–Scott–Thomson triumvirate at work. It also offers a good example of the capital investment process and poten-tial in mid-nineteenth century America. Theodore Woodruff perfected his design for a sleeping car while working as a master car-builder for the Terre Haute and Alton Railroad in Alton, Illinois. In 1856 he secured the first of many patents, scraped together a small amount of capital from his friends, and had a sleeping car built in Springfield, Massachusetts. In 1857 the New York Central allowed him a trial run at his own expense on the night express trains between New York and Albany. The experiment succeeded. Passengers liked the car and gladly paid the premium fare in order to sleep on a bed with mattresses, pillows, and clean linen, instead of stretching out fully dressed on hard benches or seats, cheek-by-jowl with sweaty hoi polloi. By 1858, Woodruff had his cars on several lines in the East and Midwest; however, his timidity and general lack of business sense limited him to car-by-car, step-by-step expansion until he approached the Pennsylvania.

Thomson and Scott immediately recognized the potential of the sleeping car and persuaded Woodruff to form a partnership with them. For propriety's sake they put their shares in Carnegie's name, and Carnegie received a chance to buy a one-eighth interest. The new partners arranged to pay for their shares in installments, a common practice in nineteenth-century finance. Investors committed themselves to pay in a specific amount of capital in a fixed number of installments over a specified period—sometimes at designated intervals, sometimes on call. This practice conferred advantages all around. If the list contained names of sufficiently elegant partners or shareholders, the firm got credit and customers more easily. (In England, businesses customarily sought respectability by trundling in an aristocrat or two.) In effect, the firm had the leverage of its total capital but paid dividends on only a fraction of it. Moreover, the managers did not have to part with any actual profits for a time, because they had the right to apply all dividends to unpaid stock subscriptions until they had collected the total amount pledged. In the mid-nineteenth century it was easy to establish a business in many industries; profitable operations could often begin quickly, and investors might never have to pony up their total subscriptions because dividends could liquidate installments. A shrewd investor could thus acquire a large interest in many firms by putting up very little money of his own. Indeed, if bold enough, or informed enough, a capitalist need not even have any money. Carnegie exploited precisely this kind of arrangement when he invested in

T. T. Woodruff and Company. He had no cash on hand, but he subscribed for his one-eighth share, "trusting," as he said, "to be able to make payments somehow or other." Less ingenuous than it might appear, he knew that his partners, Thomson and Scott, would see to it that the Woodruff cars went on the Pennsylvania's trains. He had the "big corporation" behind him.

When the first installment of $217.50 came due, Carnegie borrowed the money from a bank. But he never made another payment. In the first year, dividends paid off the entire balance; after the second year, he received $5,000 or more annually until he sold out in the early 1870s. In 1868, for example, the Woodruff investment paid $6,000. It became the cornerstone of Carnegie's fortune. It provided not only the cash—such as he needed—for subsequent investments, but also a valuable object lesson in the profitability of promoting America's economic growth. Borrowing from a bank bolstered his ego as well. As he recalled the incident, he approached the banker and "explained the matter to him, and . . . he put his great arm around me, saying, 'Why of course I will lend it. You are all right, Andy.' And here I made my first note, and actually got a banker to take it. A proud moment that in a young man's career."

He might well have felt proud. Banks at that time restricted loans largely to real estate mortgages and commercial paper with a merchant's endorsement. In the 1850s they made few unsecured industrial or personal loans. Carnegie, then only twenty-three, had his note accepted without a co-signer and without collateral; he had established an enviable reputation.

Carnegie's next major investment came in 1861 when he participated in the formation of the Columbia Oil Company. In this venture he aligned himself with William Coleman, a wealthy ironmaster and the elder statesman among Pittsburgh's businessmen. Coleman, though retired and wealthy, still restlessly pursued profitable investments. In 1861 he became interested in the oil boom then gripping western Pennsylvania. Area residents had long known about the presence of oil there, for they found it oozing out of the ground, floating on the surface of creeks, and contaminating the region's salt wells. People regarded it as a nuisance, since there appeared no way to tap the oil in quantity or refine it for use as a fuel for lamps. However, one man, Samuel Kier, found ways to make it pay. Kier had a powerful, oleaginous imagination. Capitalizing on the fact that many believed that petroleum had medicinal qualities (properties which, as Carnegie laconically noted, "vanished" when it became cheap and plentiful), he skimmed the oil off the surface of his father's salt wells, bottled it, and took to the road as a traveling medicine man dispensing Kier's Rock Oil, a cure-all of marvelous properties. This caper, while profitable, moved the oil too slowly to keep the wells clear, so Kier, mindful of the rising price of whale oil used for lamps, developed a process to distill kerosene out of petroleum, set up a refinery in Pittsburgh, and sold all he could produce.

When Edwin Drake brought in the first major producing well in 1858, the "black gold" rush at once began. Here was a dream come true: a substance pouring from the ground for which an unlimited market existed. By 1861 some wells produced three to four thousand barrels a day. Coleman and Carnegie went up Oil Creek to inspect the Storey farm on which Coleman had an option. A chaotic panoply confronted them: shanties, roads, fields, creeks, and prospectors alike were coated in oil. Feverish activity went on day and night in a carnival atmosphere. Carnegie remembered it vividly fifty years later. He had never seen anything like it:

> Good humor prevailed everywhere. It was a vast picnic. . . . Everybody was in high glee; fortunes were supposedly in

reach; everything was booming. On ... the derricks floated flags on which strange mottoes were displayed. I remember ... seeing two men working their treadles boring for oil on the banks of the stream, and inscribed upon their flag was "Hell or China." They were going down, no matter what.

Coleman and Carnegie bought the Storey farm for $40,000; it proved a bonanza. They formed the Columbia Oil Company with a nominal capital of $200,000. Investors, however, paid only $10 for each $100 share. Carnegie used his Woodruff dividends to buy 1,100 shares. This $11,000 investment returned him $17,800 the first year, and more than a million dollars altogether.

But first Coleman undertook a scheme to raise the oil's price. He ordered a huge hole dug. As Carnegie described it:

> Mr. Coleman, ever ready at the suggestion, proposed to make a lake of oil ... to hold a hundred thousand barrels ... for the not far distant day when, as we then expected, the oil supply would cease. ... After losing many thousands of barrels waiting for the expected day (which has not yet arrived) we abandoned the reserve.

After this fruitless attempt to corner the market, the company did an about-face, turning from hoarder to most efficient producer in the area. By paying high wages and by providing good tools, comfortable housing, and recreational facilities, Columbia Oil hired and kept the best drillers and roustabouts available. It became the most prosperous firm in the fields.

Carnegie learned the lesson well; production, not speculation, paid off. He was to return to this theme time and again. Altogether he found the oil business disillusioning despite the Columbia success. Subsequent ventures failed. By 1865 he had become so disenchanted that he wrote Tom Carnegie, "Sell out for cash by all means, and at once. ... Oil has seen its best days." The smell of oil made him ill all his life, and the waste offended his Scottish soul.

A messy, chaotic business, filled with wildcatters and spec-ulators, it seemed a maverick beyond the control of any management, and indeed remained so until corralled by John D. Rockefeller in the 1880s and 1890s.

Less remunerative than oil but infinitely more satisfying was his promotion of the Keystone Bridge Company, his "pet," and "the parent of all [his] other works." Here there ensued no hysterical free-for-all, with waste everywhere and profits seeping into the ground. Bridges—monuments to the genius and craft of their creators—stood forever.

The Keystone Bridge Company opened for business in 1862 assured of success. A monument to insider knowl-edge and what we today condemn as "conflict of interest," it confidently expected to do an extensive business with the Pennsylvania Railroad and lines that the Pennsylvania controlled. It numbered among its partners the following Pennsylvania officers: J. Edgar Thomson, president; Thomas A. Scott, vice-president; W. H. Wilson, chief engi-neer; Enoch Lewis, superintendent of transportation; Aaron Shiffler, bridge supervisor; J. H. Linville, bridge engineer; John Piper, supervisor of bridge construction; and Carnegie himself, superintendent of the western divi-sion. Only Piper and Shiffler left the railroad's employ. Thomson put his shares in his wife's name; Carnegie held Scott's, as had become their custom; Linville's participa-tion remained secret.

The idea of Keystone Bridge germinated from Carnegie's discussions with John Piper in 1856. Piper showed Carnegie an iron bridge being assembled to replace a burned wooden one and convinced him that iron bridges would inevitably supplant wood. Locomotive sparks often set wooden bridges on fire; moreover, the trend toward heavy trains and locomotives, in which the Pennsylvania set the pace for the industry, necessitated stronger spans. Beyond a certain load factor, iron bridges became cheaper than wood. Piper and Linville obtained several patents for their bridge designs in succeeding years and collected royalties from the railroad for their use. In 1856 Carnegie returned to Pittsburgh to become superintendent on the Pennsylvania, but he kept the bridge builders' ideas in mind. In 1862 Carnegie induced Piper and Shiffler to set up shop in Pittsburgh. Carnegie organized the partnership. The firm prospered at once, Carnegie held a one-fifth share; the initial and only assessment of $1,250 he borrowed from a bank. In 1863 Keystone paid him $7,500 in dividends and continued to do well throughout the Civil War.

When Carnegie left the railroad in 1865 he did so partly because he foresaw vast construction in the near future and determined to win Keystone a major share of it. The Civil War had interrupted railroad building. With the coming of peace, construction could recommence with fresh energy supplied by the Republican Congress's passage of the Homestead Act and legislation underwriting construction of transcontinentals. These dazzling prospects, compounded with the need to rebuild the South's railroads, brought a fever of anticipation to the industry. Freed from his railroad responsibilities, Carnegie for a time focused his efforts on the bridge company. Keystone collected fresh capital from its partners, expanded its shops, and prepared to share in the festivities.

The most exciting as well as the most profitable bridge contracts came from the need to span the Mississippi and Missouri rivers as the rails pushed westward. The transcontinental railroads generated enormous enthusiasm; they seemed to fulfill the vision of "manifest destiny"—"tying the nation together with sinews of steel," opening the vast western lands to easy settlement and assuring their prosperity by connecting them to eastern markets. In particular, the Homestead Act symbolized America's democratic heritage and powerful destiny. Even Will Carnegie, who ordinarily took little interest in

American politics, had celebrated the prospect of expanses of free land opened to settlers ("the greatest reform of the age," he called it). Now as Reconstruction began, the Homestead Act would help drive the frontier westward; behind the frontier would come railroads; and railroads would require bridges.

The biggest bridge of them all would be one across the Mississippi, and Carnegie resolved to get the contract for Keystone. As usual, he had the inside track from the start. The Pennsylvania had a major interest in the bridge and would be one of its chief customers. Using his influence with the St. Louis Bridge Company, Scott had Linville appointed chief consultant to the bridge's designer, James B. Eads. Linville then steered the contract for the bridge's superstructure to the firm in which he held a vested, albeit clandestine, interest.

The St. Louis Bridge suffered numerous delays from the outset. Eads, an eccentric genius, had no formal training in bridge design. Linville announced that the bridge, if built according to Eads's plans, would collapse of its own weight. With that the wrangle between St. Louis Bridge Company and its chief contractor began. Although authorized in 1865, construction did not get underway until 1868, and completion, originally scheduled for 1871, did not come until 1874. Exasperation prevailed on all sides as Eads revised his plans with the bridge being constructed, and Carnegie battled James Taussig, the bridge company's finance chairman, for higher prices:

> Capt. Eads must require only the custom of the trade. Anything else must be allowed for in time and money. . . . To Eads . . . this Bridge . . . is the grand work of a distinguished life. With all the pride of a mother for her firstborn. He would bedeck the darling without regards to his own or other's cost. . . . All right, says Keystone, provided he allows the extra cost and extra time.

On occasion, both Carnegie and the bridge company despaired of completion, but all persevered, and finally it was done. When it opened the Eads Bridge was the largest steel arch bridge in the world, with a center span of 520 feet. (Both builders and designers did their work well; the bridge is still in use.)

Keystone, fulfilling Carnegie's ambitions for it, continued to build most of the major new structures during the postwar boom. These included the Missouri River bridge at Omaha; the Mississippi bridge at Keokuk; the Ohio bridges at Cincinnati and at Point Pleasant, West Virginia; and a swing-bridge across Raritan Bay in New Jersey. In 1878 Carnegie capped these achievements by securing the contract for the superstructure of the Brooklyn Bridge.

Carnegie exaggerated when he called Keystone "the parent of all [his] other works"; its connection to the founding of Carnegie Steel was roundabout at best. But Keystone did serve as a testing ground for patterns of ownership and selection of managers that Carnegie followed later with good results. The firm was a partnership in which he (adding Scott's and Thomson's proxies to his own shares) held controlling interest and all key members of management held minority interests. Carnegie believed this arrangement ideal, because it gave the managers an incentive to maximize profits while assuring him of continued personal control. The multiple-member partnership—Carnegie Steel eventually had forty—was a rarity among American and English businesses. Partnership of more than three or four rarely appeared in those countries. They were, however, commonplace in Scotland in both mercantile and manufacturing firms in the eighteenth and nineteenth centuries.

Carnegie's selection of Piper and Linville as the operating chiefs also typified his subsequent strategies. These men were the undisputed experts in their field in America. Neither an engineer nor a mechanic, Carnegie knew nothing of bridge construction. He simply recruited the best talent, gave them a share in the business, and judged by the results. As long as he held the majority interest, he could control the supervisory personnel. At Keystone he developed his policy of rewarding the proficient with bigger shares and forcing out the incompetent.

Keystone rode the postwar railroad boom, which brought a 90 percent increase in railroad mileage from 1865 to 1872 as 31,000 miles of new road opened, much of it built ahead of demand, west of the Mississippi River in sparsely settled territory that offered slender prospects for early profits. This increase in trackage brought a concomitant growth in capital outlay. Total investment tripled from 1867 to 1872, reaching $3.2 billion. To amass such investment necessitated ever greater participation of outsiders, so debt financing grew even more rapidly than track mileage—it quadrupled. (Total dividends, on the other hand, only doubled. A few such shrewd observers as Charles Francis Adams and Henry Varnum Poor warned unavailingly of the ominous implications of strategies that tripled capital and quadrupled debt but only doubled mileage and dividends.) Carnegie's role as super salesman and promoter for the Keystone Bridge Company, in addition to his privileged position with Thomson and Scott, involved him in the world of high finance first in the United States and then in Europe, as American railroad and bridge promoters roamed ever further in search of capital.

Major railroad bridges, like those Keystone built across the Ohio and the Mississippi, were erected by independent firms and not by the railroads themselves. Local promoters formed a company, sold stock to finance construction, and contracted in advance to lease the finished bridge to one or more railroads. The value of the bridge company's securities, therefore, depended on the potential profitability of the railroad. The railroad often bought enough stock in the bridge company to get a voice in location, design, and construction. Such was the Scott–Linville St. Louis Bridge arrangement. On the other hand, the bridge company sometimes bought control of a railroad if it could not otherwise negotiate a contract, lest a rival syndicate induce the line to take another route, leaving the bridge high and dry. As Carnegie expressed it on one occasion:

> The control of the railroads must be absolutely ours through a majority of shares—otherwise we might be left with several millions of an investment in a Bridge, without obtaining an outlet for our traffic. It would, no doubt, be the aim of rival interests to place us in just this fix.

The construction company thus had a vested interest in helping the bridge company dispose of its securities, because no sales would mean no bridge. Usually the builders took some of their fees in securities, generally at an inflated rate. Carnegie perceived a triple potential for profit in the business: from the actual construction, from the increase in the value of the bridge securities once the line opened, and from a commission as sales agent for the bridge company's bonds. With the standard commission 2.5 percent and the total issue usually in millions, Carnegie stood to profit more from the financial transactions that preceded construction than from the actual building itself. After perfecting his sales techniques on the American markets, Carnegie then transferred his persuasive talents to a new arena—the European investment houses.

Carnegie was an ideal person to go to Europe as a bond salesman. He had the solid backing of Thomson and Scott, support which helped immeasurably, because the Pennsylvania Railroad was the darling of European investors. By 1867 he had acquired an enviable reputation as a businessman, and he was not regarded as a speculator. Nevertheless, in the next five years, he would add speculation to his list of achievements before withdrawing from the field permanently in 1872–1873.

Andrew Carnegie (left) with his cousin George N. Lauder and Thomas N. Miller, one of Carnegie's first partners in the steel business

V

The Master Moneyman:
A Fortune in Paper

Between 1867 and 1872 the craze for headlong expansion that swept the country also seized Carnegie. He became a masterful speculator, manipulating stock in Western Union and Union Pacific, jousting with entrepreneurs Jay Gould and George Pullman. He became a promoter of stocks and bonds, selling $30 million in Europe in five years. Then he abruptly abandoned his career as speculator and financier.

His personal life changed in the interval. Although he continued to dabble in the iron business in Pittsburgh, he quit his home in 1867 for a hotel suite in New York City. In 1868 he paused for a personal accounting, did not like what he found, and vowed to reform. He began to travel abroad regularly. He also continued his efforts at self-education, shifting his ground from the parlors of Pittsburgh to the salons of New York, there acquainting himself with the contemporary intelligentsia of America and Britain—Henry Ward Beecher, Herbert Spencer, Matthew Arnold, and others.

Although new intellectual experiences would greatly influence his conduct in the future, his first speculative adventures in 1867 stemmed from more mundane episodes in his past. As a telegrapher and railroad superintendent, Carnegie had early realized the earning potential of the telegraph in the growing American economy. As a maturing businessman, he appreciated the skills with which Hiram Sibley, Jeptha Wade, and Thomas T. Eckert organized the chaotic industry by absorbing company after company into Western Union. In 1863 Carnegie bought a small amount of Western Union stock; in 1867 he found an even better way to profit from the boom in telegraphy. How he did it shows another dimension of the investor's art as practiced in the rough-and-ready world of nineteenth-century commerce.

The key to profitable telegraph operation lay in railroad franchises. For telegraph companies to construct their own rights-of-way across the country would have been ruinously expensive. At the same time, most railroads preferred not to go into the telegraph business, despite their increasing dependence on the wire service. Consequently, railroads and telegraph firms entered agreements in which the latter got the exclusive right to install their lines on the railroad's right-of-way. The railroad also agreed to transport free all men and material required to build the line, to maintain it once erected, and to pay the telegraphers' wages. In return, it got free use of the telegraph, and its messages had priority over others. Without such a franchise no telegraph company could compete. By the same token, ownership of a valuable franchise sufficed to make an independent company an attractive prospective addition to a growing enterprise such as Western Union, or its principal rival in the 1860s, the Pacific and Atlantic Telegraph Company.

In 1867 a new contender surfaced, the Keystone Telegraph Company. The principal stockholders included a familiar cast of characters: Thomson, Scott, and Carnegie; as its chief asset the company held a franchise from, naturally, the Pennsylvania Railroad permitting Keystone to string two wires on the road's poles for an annual rental of $8 per mile. This franchise had two enticements. First, because the Pennsylvania had erected its own line in the 1850s at Scott's urging, the poles already stood in place; construction of the new line could finish promptly. Second, the franchise reached from Trenton and Philadelphia to the Ohio state line. Business promised to be brisk.

No sooner had this amply endowed novice appeared than a suitor presented himself in the person of James L. Shaw of Pittsburgh, the moving spirit of Pacific and Atlantic Telegraph Company. Shaw offered to exchange six thousand shares of Pacific and Atlantic valued at $150,000 for one thousand shares of Keystone with a par value of $50,000. Carnegie at once accepted, for the sellers had not paid $50,000; they had in fact paid nothing. They had simply printed one thousand stock certificates reading "par value $50" and distributed them among themselves in an agreed-on ratio. Pacific and Atlantic, on the other hand, was a going concern. Its shares had a real, current market value, as good as cash. Carnegie, Scott, and Thomson had put no money in the project; they had conjured $150,000 out of the air. Stripped of hocus-pocus, the transaction was simple: the Keystone triumvirate acted as brokers for the railroad's franchise and received $150,000 in Pacific and Atlantic stock for their pains. The Pennsylvania received $3,000 a year in new revenue and spent nothing to get it.

Shaw quickly discovered that he had gotten more than a franchise. He had acquired an aggressive new partner, for Carnegie's six thousand shares (as usual he had Scott's and Thomson's proxies) gave him a one-third interest in the firm, and Carnegie immediately pressured the company to expand. He and Scott arranged additional franchises on railroads such as the Terre Haute and Vandalia that the Pennsylvania controlled. He also formed a separate company to string telegraph wire. Once again Carnegie's insider position maximized the possibilities for his own gain.

Carnegie the major stockholder had no difficulty seeing that the Pacific and Atlantic's construction work went to Carnegie the contractor. He took his firm's fee in Pacific and Atlantic stock at the rate of $3 in shares for every $1 spent in construction on the Pennsylvania Railroad. On subsequent lines the ratio rose to five to one. With this sort of leverage, Carnegie and his allies profited greatly from dividends (37.5 percent by 1869) until 1870–1871, when Western Union's aggressive competition began to hurt them. By the end of 1872 dividends had stopped altogether, and Carnegie, demonstrating an art practiced by shrewd investors from Plymouth Plantations to Silicon Valley, fashioned an exit strategy.

Abandoning Pacific and Atlantic to its fate, Carnegie executed a nimble two-step that enabled him to dance off the sinking ship with a profit. In December 1872 he secretly arranged with Western Union to exchange six shares of Pacific and Atlantic stock for one share of Western Union. At prevailing market prices Pacific and Atlantic stockholders stood to make $13 for every six shares exchanged. (Western Union hoped thus to gain a controlling interest in Pacific and Atlantic without having to buy the firm outright.) Quietly Carnegie began exchanging his, Thomson's, and Scott's stock, while continuing to buy on the open market. By the time he got the shares all exchanged, word of the bonanza had leaked out. The price of Pacific and

Atlantic stock began to rise as speculators rushed in. At once Carnegie executed his turnabout. He and his friends had not only gotten rid of their Pacific and Atlantic shares, but they had also acquired a significant interest in Western Union in the bargain. Now flying his new firm's colors he stopped further exchanges, leaving Pacific and Atlantic's remaining shareholders to go down with the ship.

Carnegie had proved himself equally supple in his earliest major venture, the Woodruff sleeping cars. The inventor's initial success lured many rivals into the field, but he himself lacked the temerity to face aggressive competition. Gates Sleeping Car Company and Knight Cars had made serious inroads by 1862. The Wagner Palace Sleeping Car Company (with Cornelius Vanderbilt's sub rosa participation) had forced Woodruff from the New York Central. All of these competitors' cars featured such improvements as better ventilation, more effective lighting, and more comfortable beds. They infringed on patents that Woodruff himself seemed unwilling to defend.

Such passive behavior alarmed the Keystone troika. The Pacific Railroad Act of 1862 galvanized Carnegie, Thomson, and Scott into action. They decided to prepare their various enterprises for the postwar boom, and particularly for the construction and operation of the transcontinental Union Pacific. One result of this burst of activity had been Keystone Bridge; another was the reorganization of T. T. Woodruff and Company into the Central Transportation Company. The new firm had an enlarged capital, collected by adding new partners (including William Knight, an erstwhile rival). Carnegie and his partners controlled the new firm, with the usual chicanery masking the major participants, Thomson and Scott, from the public.

The unexpected duration of the Civil War delayed the transcontinental line's construction, but in 1867, when the

Union Pacific invited proposals from sleeping car companies, Central Transportation pushed forward. Unfortunately, a powerful new rival had entered the lists—George M. Pullman. Ironically, Pullman's interest in sleeping cars originated in a trip he had taken in one of Woodruff's in the 1850s. Leaving his New York home to become a house mover in Chicago in 1855, Pullman later set up shop and manufactured two crude cars by converting Chicago and Alton Railroad day coaches. The venture failed in 1858. Pullman departed to Colorado, where he shunned the glitter of the gold fields for the mundane but profitable trade of store keeping. By 1863 he had accumulated $20,000.

In 1863 Pullman returned to Chicago, again determined to manufacture sleeping cars. He now pushed toward his vision with a relentless energy not unlike Carnegie's. He sensed that sleeping cars built and advertised as "rolling palaces," lavishly decorated with curtains, carpets, fine paint, and fixtures, would have an irresistible appeal to the traveling public. He named the first car of the new design "Pioneer" and arranged a first run with Chicago's leading citizens and newspaper reporters on board. Pioneer created a sensation with its "elegant window curtains," "beautiful chandeleers," and "ceiling painted with chaste and elaborate design on a delicately tinged azure ground."

Pullman, like Woodruff, had to provide the car at his own expense in order to get a trial run. Entering service on the Michigan Central between Chicago and Detroit, it succeeded immediately. Unlike Woodruff, Pullman aggressively followed up his initial success, driving profits back into expansion, hammering at railroad executives to create new openings for his cars. By 1867 Pullman had forty-eight cars in service and wanted more. When Carnegie moved to secure the Union Pacific for

Central Transportation, he found "a lion in the path," for there lurked Pullman, stalking "what I had started after."

Carnegie sized up his man quickly and concluded that cooperation made more sense than competition. No firm that relied on the lethargic Woodruff stood much chance against the aggressive Pullman. Moreover, Carnegie sensed that beneath Pullman's armor of ruthless determination lay a vulnerable, spongy core of vanity. Accosting him on the staircase of the St. Nicholas Hotel in New York, Carnegie pointed out that by competing for the contract they diminished its value. "Well," said Pullman, "what do you propose?"

"Unite," Carnegie replied. "Make a joint proposition to the Union Pacific and form a company."

"What would you call it?"

At this crucial juncture Carnegie, certain of his man's vanity, resurrected the rabbit ploy of his childhood and told Pullman he would call their joint venture The Pullman Palace Car Company. It was a master stroke.

Seizing the bait, Pullman said, "Come into my room and talk it over."

After negotiations protracted by sundry bickering and quibbling over patent rights of the old companies and division of ownership in the new one, the Pullman Pacific Car Company emerged with a capital stock of $500,000: five thousand shares at $100 each. The printing presses rolled, and the shares were divided among Oliver Ames as trustee for the Union Pacific (2,600 shares), Carnegie and his "associates" (1,200), and Pullman (1,200). In return, Central Transportation sold its patents to Pullman for $20,000.

Carnegie now demonstrated again how to make bricks without straw. At the outset none of the three principals paid anything. Before the first payment of

$10 per share came due, Carnegie had sold enough of his shares at $45 cash each to other Central Transportation stockholders to pay for his entire subscription. In the ensuing years Carnegie quietly unloaded his Central Transportation stock and bought Pullman with the proceeds. He recognized that his own "concern was in no condition to cope with that of an extraordinary man like Mr. Pullman . . . one of the most able men of affairs I have ever known."

Like his Western Union holdings, Carnegie's Pullman stock came to him as the fruit of manipulation. His chief assets were his powerful friends, Thomson and Scott. The same potent backing propelled him into the role of overseas agent for the securities of American railroad and bridge companies. Carnegie placed over $30 million worth of these securities in all. The customary commission in such transactions was 2.5 percent, but shrewd dealers often found ways to make more than a simple, straightforward commission.

By the time Carnegie became a bond salesman, he had come a long way from the timid lad who took a flyer in Adams Express only to follow his "great man." He still followed his great man, but the stakes had grown. "Big business, Andy," Scott told him, and Carnegie sailed away to Europe with a bag full of bonds and a pocket full of letters of reference. The St. Louis Bridge Company provided the opportunity for Carnegie's first major success in placing securities overseas. Scott's influence procured for Carnegie the right to arrange the sale of $4 million in bonds. If he succeeded in placing the bonds at 85 percent or better of face value, he would receive a commission of $50,000 in St. Louis Bridge Company stock. Here indeed Carnegie flourished on the new industrial world in action—a trip across the ocean, a few hours of quiet negotiations, a handshake—and, in the words of Joseph Wall,

"That was all it took to move into the market the necessary gold to heat the foundries in Pittsburgh and put iron beams across a muddy river 5,000 miles away." For carrying the bonds on one trip to England Carnegie stood to make more than his father could have earned in several lifetimes toiling at a loom.

In March 1869 Carnegie took the St. Louis Bridge bonds to the investment banking house of Junius S. Morgan in London. The elder Morgan, an American and a former dry goods merchant long resident in London, specialized in marketing American railroad securities to British investors. Through judicious selection—aided by his son Pierpont, who remained in New York—Morgan established a reputation for dealing only in sound investments. If his house agreed to handle an issue, its sale was assured. This endorsement loomed especially valuable in 1869, for the recent rascally capers of Daniel Drew, Jay Gould, and Jim Fiske, who plunged in and out of Erie Railroad stocks, engineering corners and crashes, bribing judges and legislators, destroying the value of the Erie's securities, had given American stocks and bonds an odious reputation.

In Morgan's office Carnegie encountered Cornelius Sampson, financial editor of the *London Times*. Sampson at once brought up the subject of Gould and Fiske, pointing out that since those worthies apparently controlled the courts, no holder of American bonds would have much chance for legal redress in case of default. Carnegie glibly retorted that the St. Louis Bridge would be a "toll gate on the continental highway," and that it had a charter from the United States government. Sampson, presumably ill-informed about the character of the American government of the time, found this reassuring, because he vowed to publicize the issue favorably. Morgan, delighted with Carnegie's nimble retort, took the bonds at 85 percent.

Carnegie had earned his $50,000 in stock, but he had even bigger plans. He wrote to Frank Taussig, St. Louis Bridge Company's finance chairman, and asked to borrow $200,000 of the proceeds of the bonds at 7 percent claiming that he needed "to use the funds, just now, for the completion of the Keokuk Bridge." It was a lie. Carnegie had a better place for the money than Keokuk Bridge. Expecting Taussig's approval, he asked an associate in Pittsburgh to invest the $200,000 in short-term paper at 8 or 9 percent. Here Carnegie manifested the investors' mentality par excellence, borrowing at 7 percent to invest at 8 percent, restlessly searching, thrusting for profitable employment for idle money whether or not it was his own.

In 1870 Carnegie consummated an even more sophisticated deal in which the Allegheny Valley and Pennsylvania railroads exchanged $5 million in bonds. The Allegheny Valley Railroad received securities marketable in Europe, and the Pennsylvania saved 1 percent interest. Carnegie collected two separate commissions on $5 million. In addition, Thomson stipulated as a condition of the exchange that Carnegie be appointed selling agent for the Allegheny Valley's new securities. Carnegie placed them with Morgan at 87 percent and pocketed a third commission on essentially the same transaction.

In early 1871 George Pullman learned that the Union Pacific desperately needed $600,000 in cash. A number of eastern syndicates vied for control of the road, because they hoped to tie it into a coast-to-coast line (a dream still unfulfilled as the twentieth century draws to a close). The Union Pacific's embarrassment presented a speculator's golden opportunity. Pullman told Carnegie, who at once rushed to Thomson. Thomson gave Carnegie enough Pennsylvania stock to secure a bank loan of $600,000. This money Carnegie lent to the Union Pacific in return for several concessions. First, Scott, Pullman, and Carnegie joined the Union Pacific's board of directors. Second, Scott became chairman of the board. Third, the Union Pacific gave Thomson some $3 million of its own stock as collateral for the $600,000 loan. Finally, Thomson, Scott, Pullman, and Carnegie had the right to buy as many of these shares as they chose at the market price prevailing at the time of the loan.

Word of this astonishing *coup de main* burst like a bombshell. Carnegie and his colleagues had outmaneuvered Vanderbilt, Gould, and John Murray Forbes's Boston syndicate to win the most sought-after prize of the day. Unfortunately the triumph proved short-lived. The prospect of the Pennsylvania's support and Scott's guiding hand as board chairman (he was then considered the most able railroad manager in America if not the world) sent Union Pacific's stock climbing in the market. The temptation proved too great for the conspirators, who began unloading their $3 million in cheap stock at a handsome profit. When word of this prestidigitation leaked out, retribution came swiftly. Carnegie recalled, "Instead of being a trusted colleague of the Union Pacific directors, I was regarded as having used them for speculative purposes. . . . At the first opportunity we were ignominiously but deservedly expelled from the Union Pacific Board. It was a bitter dose for a young man to swallow."

Carnegie's last financial adventure came in July 1872. On behalf of the Davenport and St. Paul Railroad and their American bankers, Drexel, Morgan Company, he carried $6 million in bonds to Frankfurt-am-Main in Germany to the banking firm of Sulzbach Brothers. Carnegie dueled with the wily Sulzbachs for three months. Acerbic cables flew back and forth negotiating additional guarantors, third-party evaluations of the property, and other extraordinary precautions demanded by the Germans. In the end, the Sulzbachs bought the bonds. (Their caution proved justified but inadequate; the railroad defaulted without repaying a penny.)

In 1872 Carnegie's career as speculator and security salesman came to an end. He declined two further opportunities to involve himself in major speculative projects. It took little reflection to reject wheeler-dealer Jay Gould's offer to buy the Pennsylvania Railroad and install him as president. The other decision was more difficult. Tom Scott, smarting from his ejection by the Union Pacific, had embarked on the venture that eventually led to his downfall, the Texas and Pacific Railroad. He reserved $250,000 in stock for Carnegie. Carnegie felt obliged to purchase that amount, but he decided against any further participation in the ill-fated project.

Carnegie retired from the field of speculation, having demonstrated his expert grasp of yet another kind of business enterprise. Once again, at the pinnacle of success he shifted his energies to a different arena. In 1872 construction began on what became Carnegie Steel. Thereafter Carnegie concentrated increasingly on it. Thirty-seven years old, he longed to create something real, something his own. In all his speculative ventures he had felt like a parasite, a barnacle carried forward on the flank of the Scott–Thomson ship of fortune. It brought him great wealth, but an idle, passive kind of gain, obtained without the power of creation. Carnegie longed to build. "My preference was always for manufacturing," he said. "I wished to make something tangible."

Moreover, his conscience bothered him. Although he liked to describe himself as a "first-class, steady-going securities man," he often dealt in paper of dubious value and knew it. The Davenport and St. Paul and the Missouri, Iowa, and Nebraska railroads went bankrupt, as did the Keokuk Bridge. Other ventures struggled along at the edge of collapse. Later he claimed, "I have never bought or sold a share of stock speculatively in my life," but this untruthful statement sprang from his embarrassment at having done just that. At one time or another he lied, concealed information, and misrepresented the facts, all in pursuit of speculative manipulation. He managed these things with energy and skill. Excited by his growing wealth, he obviously gloried in his association with the Morgans and other moguls of high finance. In the end, however, the game palled. Speculative fever continued to sweep the country, but in Carnegie something—his Radical past, memories of the abuses of Scottish landlords, thoughts of his father, perhaps—caused him to reconsider.

Although he yearned to build, and did, he also felt uneasy with his acquisition of wealth. Below a list of his holdings ($400,000) in 1868 and the income they provided ($56,000) he wrote:

Thirty three and an income of 50,000$ per annum. By this time two years I can so arrange all my business as to make no effort to increase fortune, but spend the surplus each year for benevolent purposes. Cast aside business forever except for others.

Settle in Oxford & get a thorough education making the acquaintance of literary men—this will take three years active work—pay especial attention to speaking in public.

Settle then in London & purchase a controlling interest in some newspaper or live review & give the general management of it attention, taking a part in public matters especially those connected with education & improvement of the poorer classes.

Man must have an idol—The amassing of wealth is one of the worst species of idolitry. No idol more debasing than the worship of money. Whatever I engage in I must push inordinately therefor should I be careful to choose that life which will be the most elevating in its character. To continue much longer overwhelmed by business cares and with most of my thoughts wholly upon the way to make more money in the shortest time, must degrade me beyond hope of permanent recovery.

I will resign business at Thirty five, but during the ensuing two years, I wish to spend the afternoons in securing instruction, and in reading systematically.

Some points of this program in self-improvement he never managed to fulfill—Oxford, for example. Others were long delayed. He continued for many years to "push inordinately" and from time to time felt "overwhelmed by business cares." But finally he did "cast aside business forever, except for others." Indeed the document expressed a theme to which Carnegie later returned. Just as the boyhood letters to Dod Lauder arguing America's superiority emerged later as a publication, *Triumphant Democracy,* so did this manifesto form the basis for the famous "Gospel of Wealth" in 1889. Eventually Carnegie fulfilled his destiny as he outlined it in 1868 and 1889. The philanthropy and the retirement had to wait; he had to build first. But the education, the search for a life "elevating in its character," which had begun in Dunfermline with Uncle Lauder, Burns, and Shakespeare, continued in Pittsburgh and New York.

Wherever he was, whatever he was doing, he found time and outlets for his intellectual curiosity. As a boy in Allegheny he organized his friends—John Phipps, Tom Miller, Bob Pitcairn, Dave McCargo—into the Webster Literary Society to debate the issues of the day. He saw Shakespearean plays in the Pittsburgh theaters where he delivered telegrams. In the library of Colonel James Anderson, who lent his books to the working boys of the town, he read George Bancroft's *History of the United States,* the works of MacCaulay, Lamb, Shakespeare, and other classics.

In the 1850s his Radical bent found outlet in the abolition movement. His group began weekly discussions of
Horace Greeley's anti-slavery editorials. In Altoona,
Scott's sister introduced him to drawing room and dining
room etiquette. He learned to ride horseback. In
Homewood he made new friends and moved to a higher
intellectual plane. He met Leila Addison, who corrected
his attire, grammar, and logic. He formed a new group,
The Original Six, including Miller, Henry Phipps, and
John Vandevort, who became his companions on the pleasure jaunts he sandwiched between business trips.
Excursions with them to Great Britain and the Continent
introduced him to painting and sculpture and provided his
"first great treat in music." In the library of Niles Stokes,
general counsel of the Pennsylvania, he encountered the
inscription:

> He that cannot reason is a fool,
> He that will not a bigot,
> He that dare not a slave.

It so impressed him that he emblazoned it in his own
library forty years later.

In New York his cultural horizons broadened further.
He gravitated to the salon of Anne Lynch Botta, long the
doyenne of New York's literati. In her youth her
"evenings" had attracted Edgar Allan Poe (who gave the
first recital of "The Raven" in her drawing room),
William Cullen Bryant, Henry Clay, Daniel Webster, and
Ralph Waldo Emerson. When Carnegie met her, she was
nearly sixty. The old stars (save Emerson) had passed on
and been succeeded by a new galaxy: Andrew D. White,
Julia Ward Howe, Charles Dudley Warren, Henry Ward
Beecher, Courtland Palmer, and on occasion, Matthew
Arnold. If these luminaries glowed less brightly than
their predecessors, they nevertheless dazzled Carnegie,

who claimed that "the position of the Bottas enabled them to bring together . . . the best known people of this country [and] the most distinguished visitors from abroad."

In these New York gatherings he furthered his ambition to "get a thorough education, making the acquaintance of literary men," and to develop the philosophical underpinnings of "that life which will be most elevating in its character." Courtland Palmer sponsored Carnegie's membership in the Nineteenth Century Club where he met Abram Hewitt, George Washington Cable, Theodore Roosevelt, and others. Their discussions led him to the works of Darwin, Auguste Comte, and above all, Herbert Spencer. As Carnegie absorbed Spencer's doctrine of Social Darwinism, he recalled that:

> Light came in as a flood and all was clear. Not only had I got rid of the theology and the supernatural, but I had found the truth of evolution. "All is well since all grows better" became my motto, my true source of comfort. Man was not created with an instinct for his own degradation, but from the lower he had risen to the higher forms. Nor is there any conceivable end to his march to perfection. His face is turned to the light, he stands in the sun and looks upward.

Spencer thus revealed to Carnegie the fundamental life process in a form that made sense to him in the light of his own career. Reading Spencer did not make Carnegie successful; indeed he had already made himself twice over, as a manager and as a capitalist, before he encountered Spencer. But Spencer's philosophy reinforced Carnegie's belief that by following his own star he helped move society as a whole toward its bright destiny. Nothing less could satisfy the restless spirit of Radical independence, his Old World heritage.

The path lay open to him; he knew the way to go. He "had lived long enough in Pittsburgh to acquire the man-

ufacturing, as distinguished from the speculative, spirit."
And so, in 1872 he turned to a new career in the manufacture of iron and steel.

The Bessemer process, in a drawing from an issue of *Harper's Weekly,* published in 1886

VI

The Master Builder:
A Foundation of Iron

In 1872 Americans, at least those outside the South, had enjoyed seven years of peace and prosperity. Buoyed by optimism, entrepreneurs sought innovative ways to exploit soaring American markets. Aaron Montgomery established a retail mail-order firm in Chicago and named it after himself. Edward Simmons of St. Louis created the first mercantile corporation, the Simmons Hardware Company.

Mark Twain celebrated his western and Hawaiian adventures in the pages of *Roughing It*. In New York, self-appointed snobbery impresario Ward McCallister named a group of the city's wealthiest men "patriarchs" of the city's Gilded Age society.

Elsewhere, life took grimmer turns. Wearying of the problems of Reconstruction, Congress passed the Amnesty Act, readmitting all but a few hundred former confederates to public life and ending the Freedmen's Bureau, leaving former slaves largely on their own in the hostile South. Much of the city of Boston burned. The Crèdit Mobilier scandal erupted, exposing corruption in the construction of the transcontinental Union Pacific Railroad, much of it financed by the federal government. In a performance worthy of Carnegie, Scott, and company, Congressman Ames Oakes of Massachusetts, together with other members of the Union Pacific's Board of Directors, had formed a construction company to which they awarded most of the railroad's contracts. To ward off scrutiny into the dubious use of public money, Oakes passed out railroad stocks to congressmen and cabinet members in places where, as he observed, "it would do the most good." The scandal besmirched the reputations of many inside of government and out, though later analysts concluded that only such shady inducements could have gotten a railroad built through thousands of miles of empty prairie, alkaline deserts, and massive mountain ranges. In November, despite public outrage, Americans re-elected U. S. Grant to a second, scandal-ridden term as president.

Elsewhere, in November 1872 Andrew Carnegie formed a company to manufacture Bessemer steel. He designed the enterprise to exploit two opportunities for great profits that he had perceived while working for the Pennsylvania Railroad: the vast market for steel rails and the chance to dominate the field by applying the new cost-based management techniques to the old trade of iron manufacture. Carnegie had already made some effort to develop both ideas, but in separate enterprises. The new firm, the embryo of Carnegie Steel, marked the transition of Carnegie from capitalist to entrepreneur, a shift for which he had begun to lay the groundwork years before.

When Carnegie brought home the "golden egg" from the Adam Express goose, he and his colleagues "resolved to save and watch for the next opportunity for investment . . . and for years afterward [they] . . . worked together almost as partners." Tom Miller and Carnegie dabbled in a variety of small investments. Miller's career paralleled

Carnegie's. He too worked for a railroad, the Pittsburgh, Chicago, and Ft. Wayne, and rose to superintendent. He moved from Allegheny to Homewood, marrying one of William Coleman's daughters. He exhibited the same restless drive as Carnegie in maximizing opportunities and seeking new ones. It was he who became intrigued by the investment possibilities in iron and who first involved Carnegie in them. Carnegie cited him as "the pioneer of our iron manufacturing projects."

In 1861 Miller and Carnegie made a small investment in the Freedom Iron Company of Lewiston, Pennsylvania. Freedom Iron manufactured rails and did most of its business in the South until the outbreak of the Civil War. Like many other iron manufacturers, Freedom's principal owner, John B. Wright, found it difficult to exploit the opportunity in rail manufacturing because of his firm's limited resources. Railroads needed large quantities of iron, delivered quickly at low prices and on long credit terms. These conditions called for strong financial resources on the manufacturers' part; and the large British firms that competed eagerly for the American trade had the requisite production capacity and financial backing. Dozens of firms sprang up around the countryside—usually joint ventures between ironmasters and rail-importing merchants—but only two (Cambria Iron and Phoenix Iron) survived the 1860s; the capital problem proved insurmountable for the others. Surviving companies faced unprecedented technological and administrative problems in achieving adequate output at acceptable costs. Furthermore, it became increasingly clear after the Civil War that in the near future railroads would demand steel rails. Few American firms possessed the cash and the expertise to enter that market.

Carnegie occupied a strategic position from which to observe these developments, for the Pennsylvania Railroad led among the push for improved rails. Rails created endless headaches. They cost a great deal to buy, ship, and install. Worse, frequent defects caused expensive derailments. Many British manufacturers specialized in a particularly trashy product for export: "American iron," the cheapest quality they produced. In addition, English firms accepted American orders, promised delivery, and then postponed actual work on them while they gave priority to one of their own railway companies. The consequent delays in construction in the United States added heavily to costs. Watching the Pennsylvania grapple with all these problems, Carnegie learned both the opportunities and the pitfalls. Just six months after joining the Pennsylvania, he wrote to Dod Lauder, "You cannot supply us with iron fast enough to keep us going."

In 1862 J. Edgar Thomson decided to try steel rails on the Pennsylvania because, as the railroad's annual report declared, "The rapid destruction of iron under the high speeds and heavy locomotives now used . . . has become a subject of serious consideration." The report added that modern operations "compelled the introduction on all thoroughfares of more powerful engines. These could only be obtained by adding to their dimensions and weight, which has produced its natural result—great wear and tear of iron rails." In 1862 only England could supply steel rails. They cost $150 a ton in gold, which meant $300 a ton in the inflated wartime American currency. Thomson ordered one hundred tons and installed them at points of heavy wear—in yards and as the outside rail on main line curves, with mixed results—the rails' surfaces wore very little, but the heads broke off from many of them. Thomson concluded, nonetheless, that steel had demonstrated its potential superiority. He placed two additional orders for five hundred and one thousand tons. "The general introduction of steel rails," he declared in 1866, "is now wholly a commercial question, in which the cost of increased capital required for their purchase becomes the chief impediment to their general adoption." This situation would soon ease, Thomson thought, because "with enlarged works, increased knowledge of the ores . . . and great experience in its production, they will be successfully manufactured [in the United States] and the price very largely reduced."

Thomson's receptive attitude anchored in his commitment to cost reduction through maximizing car and train loads, or, in his own words, "the reduced cost of transportation which the introduction of steel rails will enable railway companies to afford." That heavy cars and locomotives pounded iron rails to pieces Carnegie knew as well as Thomson. As superintendent he "had seen new iron rails placed every six weeks or two months . . . upon certain curves." The Pennsylvania had committed itself irrevocably to more massive equipment; therefore, iron rails would have to go. Indeed, rails were only the beginning. Long heavy trains needed steel from end to end—in boilers, couplers, locomotive and car frames, brake shoes, and wheels.

Carnegie saw in Thomson "the great pillar in this country of 'steel for everythin'.'" As soon as the Civil War ended, Carnegie girded his enterprises for the inevitable boom. Just as he had expanded the Keystone Bridge Company to make ready for the Mississippi and Missouri river crossings, so now he concentrated on meeting the demand for steel rails. As Carnegie well knew, Henry Bessemer had found sufficient sources of phosphorus-free ore to allow British rolling mills to contemplate mass production of steel rails. These would soon appear on the American market, and other railroads would follow the Pennsylvania's example by buying them.

Hoping to steal a march on his British rivals, Carnegie returned to England in the fall of 1865, met his cousin Dod Lauder (who had by now taken a degree in engineering at Glasgow), and inspected the "Dod patented rail process." This scheme purported to fuse a steel face on iron rails, providing great strength at low cost. Carnegie helped finance the American Steeled Rail Company, which Dod established to manufacture his rails in the United States. Carnegie persuaded Thomson to try the Dod rails, but they failed embarrassingly: "During the cold weather . . . —they were removed although the ordinary Iron Rails alongside, . . . showed but little wear."

When the Dod experiment failed, Carnegie, who had gradually acquired the controlling interest, decided to convert Freedom Iron to the production of Bessemer steel. Like many other Americans, he hesitated to get involved in the patent dispute between Bessemer and the American syndicate that owned the rights to William Kelly's similar process. At times (in his sleeping car ventures, for example), Carnegie did disregard the legal complications of patents, but in this dispute, the parties showed a truculent determination to prosecute violators. Finally, in 1866, the two camps agreed to pool their patents and share royalties. Ore had also started to flow from Michigan mines; Carnegie determined to proceed.

Freedom Iron became Freedom Iron and Steel in 1866; it retooled for the Bessemer process. The changeover moved slowly; production did not begin until 1868. In the interim, the impatient Carnegie tried yet another unsatisfactory process—rolling iron rails with steel heads. Small wonder, then, that when Tom Scott urged him to invest in a new chrome steel rail process, Carnegie replied: "My advice (which don't cost anything if of no value) would be to have nothing to do with this or any other great change in the manufacture of Steel or Iron."

Freedom Iron and Steel survived, but costs kept prices so high as to preclude mass sales. By 1872 Carnegie decided that ore supplies and transportation facilities had sufficiently developed to permit expansion. In addition, he perceived that he could reduce costs by using methods perfected in his other enterprises.

At no time prior to 1872 had Carnegie acted as an innovator in the rail-manufacturing industry; rather, he performed his customary roles of capitalist and salesman. But in his other iron firms, Keystone Bridge and Union Iron Mills, he innovated energetically, and he drew on his experiences in these firms to shape the highly innovative Carnegie Steel.

Carnegie's entry into Union Mills resulted from a complicated set of quarrels and intrigues among several of his friends, of whom Tom Miller proved the most refractory. While acting as purchasing agent for the Pittsburgh and Ft. Wayne Railroad, Miller formed a partnership in 1859 with Andrew and Anthony Kloman, two German brothers who manufactured railroad axles. The Klomans needed $1,600 to install a second trip-hammer in their forge. Miller agreed to supply the money but decided not to associate himself publicly with the firm because he intended to continue funneling his railroad's orders to it. In the interests of discretion, another party would purport to hold Miller's share. Naturally Miller wanted Carnegie, but the Klomans feared his aggressiveness, so the choice fell instead to Henry ("Harry") Phipps Jr., a close friend of Tom Carnegie and the younger brother of John Phipps, an original member of the Webster Literary Society in Allegheny. Eking out a living as a bookkeeper when Miller asked him to take half his interest in the Kloman firm, Phipps had plenty of ambition but no money, so Miller advanced him the necessary $800—a modest loan that eventually yielded a $50 million fortune. Phipps became a partner and kept the firm's books in the evening.

In 1861 the Klomans sought to expand, so the company reorganized with a nominal capitalization of $80,000 "to be paid in from time to time as the wants of the business may demand." With the rush of wartime orders the firm prospered enormously. When Miller sailed to Scotland with Carnegie and his mother in 1862, he rejoiced at having made a profitable investment that actually took none of his time. With the parsimonious Phipps as accountant, he had no fear of being cheated.

Unfortunately, prosperity broke up the alliance formed in more straitened circumstances. After some acrimonious wrangling, the disputants brought in Andrew Carnegie as mediator, probably because he alone remained on speaking terms with all parties. The agreement that Carnegie negotiated reallocated interests so that Kloman held one-half, Phipps one-third, and Miller one-ninth. It also stated that Kloman and Phipps had the right to buy out Miller's interest at any time for $10,000 on sixty days' notice. Such clauses stipulating the right of partners to buy one another out at book value were common at the time; they protected survivors in the event of a partner's death. It was not, however, customary to direct the option to one partner alone. Kloman and Phipps, after saying that they would not, promptly did force Miller out of the firm. To add to the internecine complexities of the struggle, Tom Carnegie replaced Miller by buying half his interest and lending Phipps money to buy the other half.

The elder Carnegie responded to this treachery by forming a new partnership with Miller, Piper, and Linville called Cyclops Iron Works in October 1864. They erected a mill a half-mile upstream from the Kloman establishment. Soon the advantages of unification (or the perils of competition) became obvious; the two firms merged into the Union Iron Works in May 1865, Phipps and the two Carnegies outvoting the dissidents, Kloman and Miller. Unable to bear even nominal association with Phipps, his erstwhile protégé ("I could not bear the stink of such treachery"), Miller asked Carnegie to buy him out. Carnegie agreed, thereby acquiring a majority interest.

Carnegie's primary motive, first in founding Cyclops and then in merging it into Union Iron, was to create a reliable and cheap source of beams and plates for

Keystone Bridge. In other words, he integrated two successive stages of manufacturing vertically under a single
controlling head. For the first time he acted as an innovator in manufacturing, rather than as an imitator. For the
first time he attempted to increase profits by departing
from established practice rather than by excelling at it.

With the exception of a few rail mills such as Phoenix
and Cambria, in 1865 the iron industry in America
remained unintegrated. Like many manufacturing industries of the time, its organization still resembled that of the
linen trade in Will Carnegie's day. Each stage of manufacture from raw materials to finished products took place in
a separate, independent production unit, almost always a
small proprietorship or partnership. Iron furnaces smelted
the ore into pig iron; forges and rolling mills converted pig
iron to bars and slabs; other mills then rolled rails, plates,
and sheets, and cut nails. Separate factories fabricated
tools, hardware, pots and pans; foundries made stoves.

The dominant factors in the iron trade were the specialized merchants who regulated the flow of materials from
one manufacturing stage to another and then into the market. Their ability to sell combined with their superior capital resources gave them tight control of the trade, a control they still exercised when Carnegie organized Union
Iron. Merchants determined who produced what and for
how much it sold. This traditional arrangement added significantly to the cost of the final product, because middle-
men collected fees at every transfer point, and because the
movement of material proceeded slowly through many
hands and over a wide geographic area. The large quantity of material in the pipeline at any time kept a good deal
of money tied up in inventories. Invariably this was borrowed money, and the finance charges on it added significantly to the cost of the final product.

To Carnegie's railroad-trained eye this method of operation embodied multiple inefficiencies. To make money, he

knew, required speeding up the flow and getting more product through the facilities faster, the same principle as running bigger trains and running them faster to cut unit costs and to increase profits. By integrating Keystone and Union Iron, Carnegie moved in this direction.

Another realization proved equally illuminating. The novice iron manufacturer discovered that most ironmasters used bookkeeping systems unchanged since the Renaissance. Carnegie recorded in his *Autobiography*:

> I was greatly surprised to find that the cost of each of the various processes was unknown. Inquiries made of the leading manufacturers of Pittsburgh proved this. It was a lump business, and until stock was taken and the books balanced at the end of the year, the manufacturers were in total ignorance of the results. I heard of men who thought their business at the end of the year would show a loss and had found a profit, and *vice versa*.

Clearly this would not do. Tooling up a business to compete for million-dollar contracts without incorporating the ability to make accurate cost estimates might well have ended in disaster. "I felt as if we were moles burrowing in the dark, and this to me was intolerable. I insisted upon such a system of weighing and accounting being introduced throughout our works as would enable us to know what our cost was for each process." The Pennsylvania had taught Carnegie the necessity of cost control. This, principle, Carnegie realized, applied equally to manufacturing:

> One of the chief sources of success in manufacturing is the introduction and strict maintenance of a perfect system of accounting so that responsibility for money or materials can be brought home to every man. Owners who, in the office, would not trust a clerk with five dollars without having a check upon him, were supplying tons of material daily to men in the mills without exacting an account of their stewardship by weighing what each returned in finished form.

With accountability achieved "by the aid of many clerks and the introduction of weighing scales at various points in the mill," Carnegie could discover "... who saved material, who wasted it, and who produced the best results." He could thus keep track of "what every department was doing, ... what each of the many men working at the furnaces was doing, and ... compare one with another."

Thus, long before the formal elaboration of "scientific management" in the writings of Frederick Taylor and Alexander Church, Carnegie instituted a system that generated detailed cost data on units of labor and material per unit of output and applied it to management decision making. Thomson and Scott, developers of the system, had turned the Pennsylvania into the "standard railroad of the world" with it. Carnegie applied the system to iron and steel manufacturing, built the first modern industrial unit in America, revolutionized the structure of his own industry, and established the pattern that others imitated so effectively that the United States rose to world industrial supremacy. Carnegie did not create the management system he used; that honor belonged to McCallum, Thomson, Scott, and others. But he perceived its transferability to industry and successfully adapted it.

Carnegie first proved himself to be an entrepreneur when he brought cost-based pricing and management to manufacturing—a new combination. Although he had often associated with entrepreneurs—Woodruff and Pullman, Thomson and Scott, Piper and Shiffler—he had never played the part himself. In 1865 at Union Iron he began. It took time to perfect the arrangements, because, as so often happens when new methods are forced on practitioners of an old trade, Carnegie's ideas encountered resistance: "Every manager in the mills was naturally against the new system. Years were required before an accurate system was obtained." But he was determined, and he owned a majority of the firm, so he prevailed.

Under his direction cost accounting became the key factor in marketing, investment, and personnel decisions. For Keystone and Union Mills, cost data determined price more than prevailing market conditions. The basic Carnegie sales strategy, "scoop the market," depended on knowing costs with a certainty that made it possible to quote a low price with the confidence that it would yield a profit. In some situations—the St. Louis Bridge, for example—no market price existed, for there were no precedents; furthermore, when Eads demanded modifications of the original plan, the contractor's costs rose accordingly. In both cases, Keystone could set rational prices because of its ability to measure expenses.

Cost data influenced investment decisions as part of the policy of cutting cost per unit of production, first, by speeding up flow in order to produce more goods per dollar of capital; second, by cutting labor costs while maintaining production levels. Both techniques could be applied to the manufacturing processes themselves and to the intervals ("interfaces") between separate operations. Carnegie manipulated each of these variables. Cost analysis pinpointed expensive operations and facilitated decisions on whether investment in new equipment would pay off in savings. At Union Mills, his "strict system of accounting enabled [him] to detect the great waste possible in heating large masses of iron." On the basis of these data he decided to install new furnaces. He described the results:

> . . . the older heads among the Pittsburgh manufacturers [criticized] the extravagant expenditures . . . on these new-fangled furnaces. But in the heating of great masses of material, almost half the waste could sometimes be saved. . . . The expenditure would have been justified even if it had been doubled. . . . In some years the margin of profit was so small that the most of it was . . . from savings . . . from the improved furnaces.

Speeding up individual operations delivered further savings. One of the attractions of the merger between Kloman and Cyclops lay in the fact that Kloman had invented a metal saw, an upsetting machine, and a universal mill, machine tools that made it possible to fabricate iron and steel beams and plates to exact measurements at high speed. This promised a significant saving in the manufacture of Keystone's bridge parts.

The chief advantage of the merger into Union Mills, however, was the reduction in the time and labor required to move material from operation to operation. The vertical integration eliminated the middleman, coordinated operations of the integrated units, minimized inventories, eliminated duplications in machinery, and permitted the shifting of skilled workers to meet temporary needs. If all the integrated units minimized costs, the price of the final product could be held down, volume kept up, and each stage of production could show a profit. In the early years, Carnegie at times had problems keeping recalcitrant partners such as Piper and Linville pulling together. When necessary he cracked the whip and urged compliance, reminding Keystone's John Linville on one occasion, "You [and Union Mills] are not competitors; on the contrary you are necessary to each other—the true policy is to work together."

In coordinating the two units' operations, Carnegie accomplished something more difficult and of much greater economic significance than simultaneously managing separate enterprises. He built a system, that is, a logical arrangement of manufacturing operations with each stage controlled to reduce costs. Blending Union Iron and Keystone into a smoothly functioning system took time. His experiences in overcoming all obstacles convinced Carnegie that he was on the right track and that he must always have control so as to enforce his policies. Nothing ever shook these convictions. By 1870 he felt confident enough to expand. The trial period had ended.

The attractions of further integration led Carnegie to build a blast furnace to guarantee supplies of pig iron at an assured price. Construction on the furnace (called the "Lucy" after Tom Carnegie's wife, such names being the custom of the day) began in 1870. The furnace went into blast in 1872 and produced 13,361 tons. From its first day in service, the Lucy's proprietors pushed it hard, striving always to increase production. They improved the operation by rebuilding the interior. Other technical improvements reduced delays in moving material from operation to operation. For example, when slag buildup slowed down the pouring of the smelted iron, Andrew Kloman designed a slag cooler that permitted its continuous removal. Above all, the furnace crew achieved a high volume of production by "hard-driving," that is, by getting the maximum output of iron regardless of wear and tear on the furnace. Accounting showed that "hard-driving" cost less per ton of iron produced coddling the furnace, as was the British practice. The money generated by faster production more than paid for a new furnace.

Eventually the Lucy produced more than 100,000 tons a year, confounding critics who predicted bankruptcy of the firm through cannibalization of its equipment. One such, Sir James Kitson, President of the British Iron and Steel Institute, predicted "It won't last. . . . This continual work at high pressure does not pay in the end." His erroneous observation revealed the different attitudes toward labor and machinery held in the two countries. Cost accounting had few adherents in nineteenth-century British industry; manufacturers planned largely by instinct and tradition. But Carnegie planned on the basis of evidence. The British method resulted in guesswork that kept costs high; Carnegie's produced rational policy that drove costs down. An exchange between English industrialist Sir Lowthian Bell and one of Carnegie's furnace superintendents showed the conflict in thought and policy. Bell condemned the "reckless rapid rate" of hard-driving "the furnaces so that the interior of each furnace was wrecked and had to be replaced every three years." The superintendent replied, "What do we care about the lining? We think a lining is good for so much iron and the sooner it makes it the better."

The relative availability of labor had little to do with either policy; both rested on conflicting theories of cost. Machines cost less than men; Carnegie knew it and acted accordingly. Not for nothing did he learn "what each of the many men working at the furnaces was doing" and "who saved material, who wasted it, and who produced the best results." These data he studied "thus to compare one with the other." Those who produced savings—such as William Borntraeger, whose calculations led to the Siemens Furnace—he made partners. Those found wanting he mercilessly expelled.

In 1872 Carnegie visited the Bessemer plants in England, assessed the state of the industry and his own readiness, and decided to concentrate all his efforts in iron and steel. The raw materials and technology he could get. The market existed for the taking. He had an organizational structure he believed in—the partnership in which he retained a majority interest. Most important, he had shown that his railroad management theories could convert unintegrated enterprises into an industrial system. From an initial dependence on the leadership of others, he moved toward independence; his diffuse business interests he consolidated into one; and all the knowledge he had acquired as manager and as capitalist he brought to bear on the challenges he met in his new role as entrepreneur. Twice he had shown what a poor boy could do in America; the best lay just ahead.

The Edgar Thomson steel works (photographed in 1916)

VII

The Master Builder:
A Structure of Steel

In 1872 Carnegie began to contract his interests and to focus them on a single project, his new steel-rail rolling mill. By the end of 1873 he had virtually completed the transition. He had begun the policy that he later offered as a motto to aspiring businessmen, "Put all your good eggs in one basket, and then watch that basket." (This so delighted Mark Twain that he adopted it for his story *Pudd'nhead Wilson.*)

Carnegie raised the money to construct his mill and blossomed as an entrepreneur, introducing a rational operating structure while building a staff of managers. He established the mill's procedures, turned the operations over to the staff, and set about getting orders for his company. With the force of all his experiences concentrated behind it, Carnegie's firm led American manufacturing into the new industrial world of cost-based management.

Carnegie's drive began in the fall of 1872, when he organized a partnership to raise capital. The group included William Coleman, his former partner in Columbia Oil;

David Stewart, president of Columbia Oil and the Carnegies' next-door neighbor in Homewood; David McCandless, a wealthy Pittsburgh dry goods merchant and friend of the Carnegies since their Allegheny days; John Scott and William P. Shinn, president and vice-president respectively of the Allegheny Valley Railroad; Tom Carnegie, Andrew Kloman, and Henry Phipps, Carnegie's Union Iron partners; and, of course, Tom Scott and J. Edgar Thomson.

In this array of partners only one, William Coleman, specifically shared Carnegie's enthusiasm for the future of steel. The rest went along because they had general confidence in Carnegie (Stewart, McCandless, John Scott); because Carnegie persuaded them (Shinn, brother Tom, Kloman, Phipps), or because of habit (Tom Scott and Thomson). Of the firm's original capital, $741,000, Carnegie contributed $250,000, Coleman $100,000, and the others, lesser sums. Carnegie, producing "rabbit boys" before rolling a rail, named the firm Carnegie, McCandless and Company to take advantage of McCandless's good business reputation. The new mill he called the Edgar Thomson Works (known thereafter as ET) after overcoming the namesake's reluctance. When Carnegie first proposed it, Thomson had replied, "I am a little afraid, Andy, to connect my name with American steel rails. I fear they will do me little credit." He nevertheless gave way under a rain of flattery and assurance:

> Edgar Thomson . . . carried by acclamation. "Just the very thing," was the unanimous expression. . . . We all sincerely feel that this honor will be entirely upon our side. . . . We . . . assure you that there is not one of our party who is not delighted that an opportunity has arisen through which expression can be given, however feebly, to the regard they honestly entertain for your exalted character and career.

Carnegie in full cry could be extremely compelling, as partners, competitors, and the world soon learned.

With partners enlisted and christenings attended, Carnegie turned to the actual construction. William Coleman found a site at Braddocks' field on the Monongahela River, twelve miles south of Pittsburgh, that offered two main attractions. The land cost less than similar properties in Pittsburgh, and the site had access to two railroads—the Pennsylvania and the Baltimore and Ohio—as well as to river transportation. (Carnegie, an experienced rate maker himself, knew only too well what to expect should he locate his works where one railroad had a monopoly—extortionate freight rates.) Furthermore, the Monongahela and its tributary, the Youghiogheny, penetrated the coal fields of the Connellsville region, making transportation of coal and coke to the mill cheap and easy.

No sooner had construction begun than problems arose that might have deterred a less resolute man. His trials began with the Panic of 1873. When Jay Cooke's banking house, one of the country's largest, suddenly collapsed, the nation's credit structure tumbled like a house of cards, and 5,000 businesses failed within a year. Customers of Keystone Bridge and Union Iron stopped paying their bills. Some of the Carnegie, McCandless partners could not meet their commitments to the new firm. Carnegie sold his Western Union and Pullman stocks and poured the money into the mill to keep it going.

The Panic of 1873 hit Americans hard with a deeper and longer-lasting depression than any they had experienced before. Changing conditions, moreover, intensified the impact, for the recession crippled the industrial economy. As some 12,000 firms failed in a six-year period, manufacturing growth, underway for a decade, stopped dead. Factory production did not again reach 1872 levels until

1878; manufacturing employment likewise reversed to the extent that factories provided only the same number of jobs in 1879 as they had in 1869. With personal savings swept away by bank failures, unemployed urban workers faced an indefinite loss of income in an America where such social safety nets as unemployment compensation, welfare, and aid to families with dependent children did not yet exist. Many of those who could returned to the family farm, and some immigrants retreated to their mother country, but for those who could do neither, the blighted urban landscape presented bleak prospects, especially in winter. In this atmosphere, so grim for so long, seeds of discontent emerged, rooted in fears that the long-dynamic American combination of democracy and capitalism—in which Carnegie later gloried in his book *Triumphant Democracy*—might have lost its capacity to sustain growth and rising standards of living, and that big businesses might further enrich the wealthy at the expense of the poor. During the depression and the years that followed, more and more Americans—farmers, not just factory workers, but also owners of small businesses, managers, and even some capitalists—came to think the hitherto unthinkable: that to maintain economic justice in the emerging industrial economy, government would have to take an active, interventionist role.

In fact, the Panic of 1873 distressed rich as well as poor. In the midst of the turmoil Tom Scott summoned Carnegie to Philadelphia and presented him with a fresh crisis. Scott and his associates had carried forward construction on the Texas Pacific Railroad by borrowing money for short terms at high interest rates. The gamble had backfired; the creditors now wanted their money. Only if Carnegie added his endorsement to the notes would lenders renew the loans. Without his help, Scott, his friend, benefactor, and longtime partner, faced ruin and disgrace. "It was," Carnegie said, "one of the most trying moments of my whole life." Yet he had no doubts about what he must do: "I declined. . . . I was not tempted for a moment to entertain the idea of involving myself . . . nothing in the world would ever induce me to be guilty of endorsing the paper . . . of any other concern than our own firm."

Therein lay the danger. Carnegie, McCandless and Company was a partnership, not a corporation with limited liability; therefore, all partners shared responsibility for obligations incurred by any one of them. If the Texas Pacific went bankrupt (and it did), Carnegie's endorsement would drag all his partners and the Edgar Thomson down in the wreckage. He owed Scott a great deal, but not that much.

Thomson urged Carnegie to reconsider: "You of all others should lend your helping hand." If Carnegie could not himself help, he should use his influence with the Morgans. "Scott," Thomson said, "had acted upon faith in his guiding star, instead of sound discretion" but still "should be carried." Carnegie would have none of the "guiding star" foolishness: "I told Mr. Scott I had done my best to prevent him from beginning to construct a great railway before he had secured the necessary capital. I had insisted that thousands of miles of railway lines could not be constructed by means of temporary loans."

His refusal cost him Scott's friendship but saved his credit. After the confrontation with Scott, Carnegie rushed back to Pittsburgh to face an inquisition by the president and directors of Pittsburgh Exchange Bank. The bank had advanced Keystone Bridge and Union Iron large sums against their accounts receivable and feared that if Carnegie had involved himself in the Texas Pacific debacle their advances might never be repaid. Obviously expecting the worst, President Schoenberger asked his questions. The pleasure Carnegie derived from his replies was no doubt enhanced by the cost he had paid to make them: Yes, he had an interest in the Texas Pacific, $250,000 worth of stock. No, he had not borrowed a penny; he owned it outright. Yes, his friend Scott had asked him to endorse notes. But he had refused. He could not make his partners and his creditors parties to Scott's misfortune, cost him what it might. He had no debts except the routine ones of current business, and he had more than enough assets to liquidate them all at once if need be.

Having allayed the bankers' fears about his solvency, Carnegie then delivered a brief sermon on the evils of speculation in general and note endorsement in particular. The incident, Carnegie believed, remade his image as a businessman.

> Up to this time I had the reputation in business of being a bold, fearless, and perhaps somewhat reckless young man. Our operations had been extensive, our growth rapid, and . . . I had been handling millions. . . . I was apparently somewhat of a dare-devil . . . to the manufacturing fathers of Pittsburgh.

The situation now reversed itself. "The fright . . . gave place to perhaps unreasoning confidence. Our credit became unassailable."

His firm soon needed that credit. Scott and Thomson, not surprisingly, wanted to withdraw; Carnegie bought them out. Andrew Kloman, less scrupulous of his partners' rights than Carnegie, involved himself in speculative enterprises that collapsed; he too had to be bought out before the creditors could sue.

The combination of increased demands and diminished income finally brought construction to a halt. To get it going again, Carnegie sailed to London where he sold $400,000 in bonds to Junius Morgan. Carnegie hesitated to mortgage his firm before it turned a wheel, but he preferred that to diluting ownership by taking in new partners. From the first he had had a larger share than any other member of the firm. He wanted a majority, and with attrition at work he had advanced toward that goal.

Furthermore, he had advance estimates of costs and prices and had no doubt the firm could pay off the bonds quickly. Morgan must have thought so as well; he lent the money despite the panic and recession.

Morgan's money permitted completion of the Edgar Thomson Works in 1875. By pushing on with construction during the depression when labor and materials came cheap, Carnegie got the entire mill—including workers' housing—for $1.25 million, a saving of 25 percent compared to normal times. Meanwhile, the Pennsylvania legislature, frightened by the chain reaction of partnership bankruptcies during the recession, passed a law in 1874 allowing partnerships to acquire limited liability. Carnegie, McCandless immediately reorganized as the Edgar Thomson Steel Company, Limited. Relieved of dangers from that corner, Carnegie chafed to get started, confident that he had obtained the most modern and efficient works money could buy. He had made sure of this by hiring Alexander Holley, the foremost expert on Bessemer steel works, to design the plant, supervise its construction, and get production underway.

Holley brought a wealth of experience to ET. A "Renaissance man" whose talents included poetry and journalism as well as engineering, and one of the first Americans to grasp the significance of the Bessemer method of converting iron to steel, he purchased the American patent rights and designed many kinds of machinery to make the process economically viable. Before Carnegie hired him, Holley had already advanced far along the Bessemer steel learning curve by building plants at the Albany Iron Works in Troy, New York; Pennsylvania Steel in Philadelphia; Bethlehem Iron in Bethlehem, Pennsylvania; Jones and Laughlin in Pittsburgh; Joliet Steel in Illinois; and Cambria Iron in Johnstown, Pennsylvania. In fact, practically the entire American Bessemer steel industry had taken shape under

Alexander Holley's guidance. Edgar Thomson Steel thus secured the services of not only the most talented Bessemer engineer available, but also one who brought with him all the lessons learned in building the competitors' plants.

Once he had enlisted the talents of the finest construction engineer in the field, Carnegie assembled the operating staff. He had definite ideas about what he wanted—people familiar with and enthusiastic about cost accounting and cost control. The chairman, McCandless, served a primarily cosmetic function; he played a small part in actual operations. For operations chief (general manager) Carnegie chose William P. Shinn, noted for his knowledge of accounting. Holley supplied in a stroke the vital link in the chain of command, the works superintendent, a decision that proved to be as important to the Carnegie success as anything else, for the man he hired, Captain Bill Jones, gained renown as the greatest steelmaker in the world.

Captain Bill Jones (he won the rank in the Civil War and answered to it proudly ever after), the son of a Welsh immigrant, learned his trade at the Lehigh Crane Iron Works at Catasauqua, Pennsylvania, one of the first companies in America to use anthracite in place of charcoal for smelting ore. From Crane, Jones moved to Cambria as a machinist. There too he found a progressive environment, for George Fritz, the Cambria superintendent, had pioneered the development of vertically integrated rail mills and kept the company in the forefront of iron technology. Jones served as Holley's chief assistant in Cambria's Bessemer installation. Jones's departure for ET soon proved a colossal loss to Cambria. A strike shut down the plant; Captain Bill raided Cambria's staff, bringing to ET Captain Thomas Lapsley, head of the rail mill; John Renard, superintendent of the Bessemer convertors; Tom James, superintendent of machinery; Thomas Addenbrook, head furnace builder; F. L. Bridges, superintendent of transportation; and C. C. Teeter, the chief clerk.

Holley and Jones saw to it that the Edgar Thomson started with experienced superintendents and department heads, although not handpicked by Carnegie himself. In later years a myth grew up that Carnegie had a "sixth sense" for picking men. One of his partners called Carnegie "the least analytical of mortals," declaring that he chose people instinctively, often selecting those who had failed previously and turning them into geniuses. In fact, the reverse was true. Carnegie made his choices carefully, analytically: he hired the best man whatever the cost in wages because he realized, "There is no labor so cheap as the dearest in the mechanical field."

Another cornerstone of Carnegie's success lay in his use of systematic analysis to evaluate his men's performance—the first manufacturer to do so. Just as on the Pennsylvania Railroad, just as at Union Iron, Carnegie, McCandless kept individual records of "who produced the best results," "thus to compare one [man] with the other," in order to inspire what Daniel McCallum had called "an honorable spirit of emulation to excel" and to ensure "that merit and training [exerted] the most potent of all influences in giving positions of every kind." Thus Carnegie said of a suggested promotion: "He may be just the man we need. Give him a trial. That's all we get ourselves and all we can give to anyone. If he can win the race, he is our race-horse. If not, he goes to the cart." Those who turned out to be "race-horses" could aspire to promotion, even partnership. As Carnegie said, "Mr. Morgan buys his partners, I raise my own." William Borntraeger, who introduced the money-saving Siemens Furnace, understood the policy ("What we haf to do is get brices up and costs down") and eventually became a partner; Francis Lovejoy came as a telegraph operator and rose to partnership through unusual abilities as an accountant. Altogether some forty men rose through the ranks to a share of ownership. The system also fostered jealousy, bitterness, and, sometimes, despair. But it produced results.

Because Carnegie had a system of management, he could institute it at the outset, confident of judging subsequent performance rationally, rather than trusting to instinct or luck. First he chose the incomparable Holley to build his mill. Next he chose Shinn for his understanding of cost-based management. He then accepted Holley's judgment on Jones and saw to it that the plant's internal organization made sense. During the planning stages, Shinn showed him an organization chart that "divided the works into two departments and [gave] control of one to Mr. Stevenson . . . and control of the other to a Mr. Jones," Carnegie instantly recognized the flaw in this arrangement. "Upon no account could two men be in the same works with equal authority. An Army with two commanders-in-chief, a ship with two captains, could not fare more disastrously than a manufacturing concern with two men in command upon the same ground, even though in different departments." He then told Shinn, "I do not know Mr. Stevenson, nor do I know Mr. Jones, but one or the other must be made captain and he alone must report to you."

Here Carnegie demonstrated his understanding of one of the bedrock principles of modern industrial organization—the necessity to define and assign authority and responsibility so as to permit assessment of individual performance. In his father's world and in his own early career, appointment to positions of responsibility usually depended on family ties, friendships, or sponsorship. In modern industrial enterprises, the size of the workforce necessitates hiring strangers as workers and as managers. Growing firms often flounder at the point when success dictates a shift to a new management structure, as witness the struggles of late-twentieth-century firms such as Apple Computer and the Polaroid Corporation.

Carnegie, McCandless's new mill would debut as much the largest firm Carnegie had ever owned, but he approached the task of managing confident that his experience at the largest, most efficiently managed enterprise in the world had prepared him well for the task. Consequently, at the Edgar Thomson Works Carnegie turned over the operations of the most modern steel plant in the world to a staff almost entirely unknown to him, certain that his management system would allow him to set policy, assign its implementation to others, and judge the results precisely, even during his absences. Such a bureaucratic structure carried with it the penalties of anonymity, perhaps, but it could control a complex industry effectively.

Carnegie had a simple business policy, which he never abandoned: first, "Cut the prices; scoop the market; run the mills full"; second, "Watch the costs and the profits will take care of themselves." Having designed a structure to run the mills full while controlling the costs, Carnegie assigned himself the dual role of watchdog of overall performance and supersalesman. His success as a salesman rested on his ability to see changes in the market far enough in advance to meet them, on his knowledge of the railroad industry and its major figures, and on the low cost of his product.

Although Carnegie created the Edgar Thomson Works to roll steel rails, he never lost sight of the nonrailroad market. In 1876 he persuaded the Philadelphia Centennial Exposition to build half of its main exhibition out of iron and steel and to give the contract to Keystone and Union. In 1878 he got the contract to supply steel for the Brooklyn Bridge. In 1885, discerning that cities would provide the next major outlet for steel products, Carnegie converted the newly acquired Homestead Works from the rolling of rails to the rolling of structural beams and angles. Homestead beams formed the skeleton of the first skyscraper office building in America, the Home Insurance Building in Chicago. Carnegie beams went into the Washington Monument and the elevated railroads in New York and Chicago. The fact that cities replaced railroads as chief consumers had a dramatic effect on the products: in thirty years rails fell from two-thirds to one-third of the steel market. Carnegie anticipated the transition and moved to meet it but still maintained his share of the rail market.

Operations began at the Edgar Thomson Works in September 1875 with an order for two thousand rails from—appropriately enough—the Pennsylvania Railroad. A less auspicious time one could scarcely have imagined; railroads laid fewer miles of track that year than any other between 1866 and 1895. As one businessman of the time testified later, "From 1875 to 1879 you could not give away a rolling mill." Despite these difficulties, Carnegie, following his policy of "scooping the market," sold enough rails to keep his mills running full. Other rail mills had agreed to hold the price at $70 per ton; Carnegie sold his rails at $65 per ton on the basis of his data. Holley's preliminary cost estimate came to $69 per ton, but raw material prices fell enough to justify a lower price. It paid off at once—costs averaged $56.64 a ton for the first two months. Operations netted a $29,000 profit in the same period. Costs continued to decline and Carnegie continued to sell. In the summer of 1876 Carnegie wrote Junius Morgan: "[W]e have made a wonderful success—every sanguine prediction I have made is more than verified and we are making . . . rails for less than $50 per ton."

Carnegie attacked the sales problem vigorously. He knew personally virtually every important railroad official in America. He followed the long-standing practice of rolling stock manufacturers by collecting testimonial letters, reprinting them, and mailing them out to prospective customers all over the world. He never missed a chance—at shipboard press conferences when he traveled abroad, at gatherings for distinguished visitors such as Matthew Arnold—to advertise his rails, *American* steel rails, as good as England's finest. It got him publicity, it sold his rails, and he loved it. He gloried in the spotlight, and he particularly enjoyed twisting the tail of the British lion, pointing out what he, a poor immigrant Scots boy, had done in the land that had abolished "privilege." "The old nations of the world creep on at a snail's pace," he trumpeted in *Triumphant Democracy* (1886); "the Republic thunders past with the rush of an express."

Behind the scenes he worked equally hard, playing the big fish with the skill developed in years of practice. He later told the Stanley Committee (which investigated the formation of United States Steel) how he did it. He used the power of old friendship:

> For instance I want a great contract for rails. I remove to New York. Sidney Dillon, of the Union Pacific, was a personal friend of mine. [Collis P.] Huntington [president of the Southern Pacific] was a friend. Dear Butler Duncan . . . was a friend. Those and other men were presidents of railroads.

And the remembrance of things past:

> The Union Pacific had advertised for 70,000 tons of rails, the biggest order that had been given. It was to be decided at Omaha, and all my competitors, all these agents of corporations were out at Omaha, and those bids were to be opened. I walked over to Sidney Dillon. I was able to do the Union Pacific a favor once and I did it. I said, "Mr. Dillon, I want you to do this for me: your people are out there bidding on 70,000 tons of rails. I ask you to give me those rails, and I promise to take the lowest price that is bid." "All right, Carnegie."

And the old-country tie:

> Take Butler Duncan who is a fellow Scotsman. He would no
> more have given anybody a rail but me than anything in the
> world.

And of course, money:

> Take Huntington; you know C. P. Huntington. He was hard
> up very often. He was a great man but he had a great deal of
> paper out. I knew his things were good. When he wanted cred-
> it I gave it to him. If you help a man through that way, what
> chance [did] any paid agent [have]?

And the competition?

> It was absurd.

Beneath the braggadocio lay a cold, hard realism.
Carnegie could "take the lowest price that is bid" sight
unseen only because he knew that he had the lowest costs
in the industry and could make a profit at any competitor's
price. He stung the competition into quick action. The
Bessemer Steel Association invited Carnegie to a meeting
in Philadelphia "for the purpose of considering questions
connected with the trade." Translated, this statement
meant that the "Fathers in Israel" (as Carnegie liked to call
them; most of them were in fact Quakers) wanted to set up
a pool; that is, an agreement to fix prices and divide markets.

Pools, an old strategy in the American iron industry,
dated back to the 1830s when the boiler-plate mills of
eastern Pennsylvania had formed an association to keep
prices high. Pools rarely lasted, shattered invariably by the
same force that called them into being: greed. Carnegie
knew the game inside out; the Pennsylvania Railroad had
bought lots of boiler plate.

At the meeting Carnegie confronted the moguls of
the industry: Samuel Felton of Pennsylvania Steel; E. Y.

Townsend and Daniel Morrell of Cambria; Joseph Wharton of Bethlehem: Walter Scranton of Scranton Iron and Steel; and Benjamin Jones of Jones and Laughlin. These worthies had the market shares already divided up: Cambria 19 percent, Pennsylvania 15 percent, and so on. The Edgar Thomson Works was relegated to last place—9 percent. Carnegie leaped to his feet and made a speech:

> I informed each of the other representatives, all Presidents of their companies, that I was a stockholder in their concerns and as such had access to their financial reports. I singled out each president and said, "I find that you receive a salary of $20,000 a year and expenses of $80,000," etc.—instancing each one, telling him just what his salary was, and how much he spent in expenses, etc.

None of that extravagance at ET he told them. The president got $5,000 a year and no expense account; furthermore, he could "roll steel rails at $9 a ton." Moreover, he threatened to withdraw from the pool and undersell all of its members if Edgar Thomson Company did not receive a share as large as anyone's. The Bessemer Association acquiesced, a move that showed its rudimentary knowledge of costs. Carnegie's actual costs at that time ran $50 a ton. The $9 was sheer bluff, but none of the competitors dared call it. In fact, Carnegie was already underselling the others and had no intention of remaining tied to any pool.

Carnegie despised pools. He joined them periodically, usually in an attempt to get an estimate of his competitors' costs. He stayed in only as long as his share provided enough business to "run full." Otherwise, pools cost him money. As he told Abram Hewitt of Trenton Iron and Steel: "I can make steel cheaper than any of you and undersell you. The market is mine whenever I want to take it. I see no reason why I should present you with all my profits." Pools also offended his competitive spirit. He fought for the joy of winning. The first pool meeting he attended would be his last, he claimed. All in all, pools rarely worked well or long. Carnegie's protégé Charles Schwab later told a congressional committee of his experiences with Carnegie Steel:

> I went into this business in 1880, and for the next twenty years I heard of agreements [pools] of this sort every few months in some direction. Most of them were never consummated, many of them lasted a day, some of them lasted until the gentlemen could go to the telephone . . . and some of them lasted a longer period.

Carnegie had no doubts about the proper course in dealing with pools. He roamed far and wide seeking orders and taking them at any price. When Shinn informed him that "the Cambria people are becoming very bitter against us for making . . . unnecessary concessions in prices," Carnegie retorted, "Of course Cambria is bitter—she has herself to blame. . . . Let us manage our own business—take orders whenever a fair profit is secure." He added:

> Two courses are open to a new concern like ours—1st Stand timidly back, afraid to "break the market" following others and coming out without orders to keep our works going. 2nd To offer certain large consumers lots at figures which will command orders—For my part I would run the works full next year even if we made but $2 per ton.

Since his "part" constituted a majority, that's just how it was done, although profit usually exceeded $2 a ton. Carnegie got the orders; the works ran full and grew larger. In 1873, the first full year of operation, ET produced 21,674 tons of steel; in 1889, 536,838 tons, nearly 25 times the first year's output. At the same time, the cost of making rails at ET fell from $58 to $25 per ton, because, while Carnegie reached out with one hand to grasp the market, he constantly hammered at costs with the other, aided by Holley's technology as well as by the depression, which created a surplus of skilled workers available at low wages. Altogether, Carnegie managed a successful launch of his new and greatest venture despite the inauspicious circumstances of the times.

The triumphant return to Dunfermline: Andrew Carnegie (whip in hand) and his mother Margaret, seated beside him

VIII

The Master Manager:
Costs, Chemistry,
and Coke

In the seventeen years from 1872 to 1889 Andrew Carnegie yoked his management system to his sales abilities, built an integrated industrial complex with a diversified product line, and became the best-known manufacturer in the world. He continued his world travels; he published three books. He devoted increasing attention to the humanistic concerns voiced in his 1868 self-appraisal, widening his acquaintances with intellectuals and statesmen. He began a program of philanthropy and publicly proclaimed the intention to give away his fortune.

During the 1880s, as the hunger for power and the need to prove himself abated, he began to consider retirement. He found a wife for his home and a successor to run his business. At the age of fifty-four he surveyed the world from the top, convinced that proper distribution of his wealth would confirm his allegiance to the creed of egalitarianism he had espoused since boyhood. He built his fortune in rails and girders and beams that made the country strong, not through stock jobbing that drained its energies. He found great satisfaction as "a manufacturer, not an adventurer."

Always a hard taskmaster, Carnegie built the Edgar Thomson Works in the face of the country's worst depression to date. He made sales when supposedly no customers existed, and he made them yield a profit. To Carnegie, only one way could guarantee this—holding down costs.

Carnegie and his managers assaulted the problem on several fronts. They drove output up, thereby cutting unit costs across the board. They pruned areas of excessive expense both in specific manufacturing operations and in the links among them. They tried to reduce labor costs by holding down wages and substituting machines.

Cost accounting at Edgar Thomson Works began with Alexander Holley's preproduction estimates. Holley knew the fundamental importance of accounting to systematic management. In addition to extensive experience in the steel industry, he had a strong background in railroads. During the 1850s he served as technical editor of Henry Varnum Poor's *American Railroad Journal,* and with Zerah Colburn had written a treatise on the relative costs of various types of locomotives and roadbeds, one of the first works of its kind. Holley knew what Carnegie required in the way of scales, checkpoints, and the like. He and W. P. Shinn, the first general manager, spoke the same language.

Shinn adopted a voucher system of accounting similar to the one used on the railroad. Every bit of raw material, waste, and product got weighed and accounted for, as did all tools and building materials used in construction and repairs. "There goes that _____ bookkeeper," said one workman. "If I use a dozen bricks more than I did last month, he knows it and comes round to ask why." Every week—or more often in problem areas—all departments correlated their data into cost sheets that showed the cost of all operations and raw materials to the fraction of a cent per ton of output. Carnegie demanded such precision from the outset; he had "learned from [his] experience in the iron works what exact accounting meant." It took manpower but the results merited the extra work because there was "nothing more profitable than clerks to check up each transfer of material from one department to another in process of manufacture."

The system worked well from the beginning. Carnegie related proudly, "So perfect was the machinery, so admirable the plans, so skillful were the men selected by Captain Jones, so great a manager was he himself, that our success was phenomenal." The first month's operations showed a profit of $11,000, which Carnegie thought unique in the history of American manufacturing. Equally remarkable was the fact "that so perfect was our system of accounts that we knew the exact amount of profit." They quickly located potential savings. Shinn and Jones discovered, while poring over the cost sheets "to find some detail capable of judicious pruning," that broken ingot molds (into which the Bessemer converters poured molten steel) added 60 cents to the cost of each ton of steel. Experiments soon developed molds that cut the cost to 15 cents, a saving that quickly amounted to $40,000 a year.

Carnegie's watch on costs never let up in his twenty-five years in the steel business. He grew more fanatical as years passed and competition stiffened. On one occasion in the 1890s, Carnegie asked his friend Frank Doubleday, a publisher, "How much money did you make last month, Frank?" Doubleday replied that he did not know; in his business, firms drew up statements only once a year.

"Do you know what I would do if I were in that kind of business?" Carnegie asked.

"No, what?"

"I would get out of it."

Carnegie demanded equal dedication from his managers. "Carnegie never wanted to know the profits," Charles Schwab related. "He always wanted to know the cost." He ordered the cost sheets sent to him weekly wherever he was. He scrutinized them and fired off comments:

> I cannot understand *Lime*, 13 tons of lime used to each ton of metal. It can't be lime, that is certain, half-rock—I suspect.

questions:

> I am surprised at two items in cost. Coke ½ ton per ton rails— 8 bushels should smelt the pig and certainly 4 bushels the spiegel. How do you account for the rest?

and exhortations:

> Show me your cost sheets. It is more interesting to know how well and how cheaply you have done this thing than how much money you have made, because the one is a temporary result, due possibly to special conditions of trade, but the other means a permanency that will go on with the works as long as they last.

Bill Jones, who had an independent spirit and an unassailable position, liked to parody Carnegie's comments on the cost sheets:

> Puppy dog number three, you have been beaten by puppy dog number two on fuel. Puppy dog number two, you are higher on labor than puppy dog number one.

Carnegie, however, remained undeflected from his course:

> I have known from the first that our hope for profit lay for some time to come in the fact that our cost was less than others.

Carnegie also realized that such vigilance had to continue; the ET's very success made it harder to continue to succeed, for as Carnegie reminded his managers, "We must not lose sight of the fact that the great products now made must affect prices [by flooding the market]." In addition to urging on his staff, he himself searched for ways to save. Combing through the cost sheets, for example, he noted that fire insurance on the buildings cost so much that they could save money by replacing all the wooden structures with iron. He ordered it done forthwith, then canceled all insurance policies and never carried another.

The system of management allowed Carnegie to control his firm's complex operations and make intelligent decisions about promotions and firings even though he had "no shadow of claim to rank as inventor, chemist, investigator, or mechanician." One of his managers later remarked, "You [were] expected always to get it ten cents cheaper the next year or the next month." Carnegie lacked scientific understanding of the chemistry of new techniques, but he could tell if one month's costs turned out lower than another's. Similarly, he could not judge the scientific merits of the technical excuses with which a manager might cover his failure, but he could and did compare the man's performance with others in the same position. He then demanded explanations in plain English.

Henry Phipps thrived under this. He had no specific duties in the Edgar Thomson Company, but blast furnaces had attracted him from the start, and he made the Lucy Furnace his special concern. His penny-pinching soul responded to Carnegie's incessant cries for economy. Phipps noticed that the furnace men threw away the flue-cinder from the blast furnace. He found this curious, because the charge put into the blast furnace included another kind of cinder from puddling furnaces, a by-product of converting pig iron to wrought iron. He took the flue-cinder to a chemist for analysis and found that it would serve even better than puddle-cinder. The Lucy Furnace practice of throwing out flue-cinder reflected tradition, not fact. On the basis of his new knowledge, Phipps bought flue-cinder from ET's competitors at 50 cents per ton and sold puddle-cinders at $1.50, thus improving the Lucy's product and saving money at the same time.

Phipps uncovered a similar waste in the rolling mills. As the steel passed through the rollers, tiny pieces were scoured off and accumulated on the floor. It had long been the custom to throw this mill scale out. Phipps had it tested and found it was high-grade steel. He refed it to the furnaces and instructed his agents also to buy up this "waste" from competitors.

These experiences showed Phipps that the firm needed a full-time chemist, and he convinced Carnegie. Carnegie described the results:

> We found . . . a learned German, Dr. Fricke, and great secrets did the doctor open up to us. [Ore] from mines that had a high reputation was now found to contain ten, fifteen, and even twenty per cent less iron than it had been credited with. Mines that hither to had a poor reputation we found to be now yielding superior ore. The good was bad and the bad was good, and everything was topsy-turvy. Nine-tenths of all the uncertainties of pig iron making were dispelled under the burning sun of chemical knowledge.
>
> What fools we had been! But then there was this consolation: we were not as great fools as our competitors. . . . Years after we had taken chemistry to guide us [they] said they could not afford to employ a chemist. Had they known the truth then, they would have known they could not afford to be without one.

With this new knowledge the firm could exploit cheap ores and bypass expensive ones. A second Lucy Furnace went into service in 1877. For some years, said Carnegie, blast furnace operations remained "the most profitable branch of our business, because we had almost the entire monopoly of scientific management."

Carnegie's attention to costs resulted in increased use of modern techniques. Just as bureaucracy replaced personnel policy based on familial ties and patronage, so chemical research replaced ingrained habit with scientific accuracy. Carnegie's firm kept close watch on scientific developments in steelmaking on both sides of the Atlantic, never hesitated to invest in better processes or machines, and translated these improvements into greater output at lesser costs. Captain Bill Jones told the British Iron and Steel Institute in 1882 that as fast as British, French, or German metallurgists discovered new processes, "We have swallowed the information . . . and have selfishly devoted ourselves to beating you in output."

Carnegie's firm thus profited from one of the phenomena of the late nineteenth century—the reversal of the historic relationship between science and technology. In the past, science had in effect waited for technology to provide it with such needed tools for research as accurate measuring instruments, indispensable to the scientific method of research. Business saw science as a market, albeit a small one, for specialized products of metal and glass, not as a source of products or methods to manufacture them more efficiently. Manufacturing was regarded as an art, not a science. By the last third of the nineteenth century, sciences such as chemistry and metallurgy had the potential, as Carnegie's experiences showed, to make a massive positive impact on profits by improving manufacturing processes. Guided by Phipps, Carnegie led his firm down a path that many would follow with increasingly dramatic results in fields such as electricity and petrochemicals in the nineteenth century and ultimately into virtually the entire business spectrum in the twentieth. The new methods had dramatic implications, not only in terms of profits, but also in transforming manufacturing from an art to a science and wresting control of the workplace and work processes from the hands and minds of those who toiled there.

The adoption of the Thomas Basic Process typified ET's eager attention to the new scientific developments. The

Bessemer process of making steel (blowing air through molten pig iron to burn out carbon) worked only if the pig iron contained virtually no phosphorus. The Americans had a considerable supply of such ore; the British did not. The problem of making steel with high-phosphorus ore attracted the attention of Sidney Gilchrist-Thomas, a London police-court clerk who dabbled in chemistry. Improbably, Thomas found a cheap and simple answer: lining the vessel with lime, which drew the phosphorus out of the molten pig iron. Thomas announced his find at the British Iron and Steel Institute meeting in 1878. The assembled titans ignored him. Rebuffed, Thomas sought out Alexander Holley. Holley saw the process in action and arranged for a test in an English mill. The test proved Thomas's method practicable, and it soon went into commercial production at the world's largest steel mill in Eston, England.

Thanks to Holley, Carnegie heard of the Thomas process while in England in 1879, observed it at Eston, and got Thomas to sell the American rights for $300,000. It took Carnegie two years to arrange the sale to the Bessemer Steel Association, but he did so on terms that flashed the old Carnegie form. The Bessemer Association paid $275,000 for the rights; but Carnegie's firm got exempted from its share of the fee as a reward for Carnegie's services. To put the frosting on Andy's cake, Thomas paid him a $50,000 commission for arranging the sale.

To maximize the savings potential of scientific discoveries such as the Thomas process, manufacturers had to back up metallurgical and chemical discoveries with the necessary plumbing and hardware. Often this meant scrapping existing equipment, which many industrialists were loath to do. The Thomas process proved more effective in open-hearth furnaces (which in effect boiled away rather than burned out impurities) than in Bessemer converters. Many steel magnates resisted the change. But not Carnegie. He had had an open-hearth furnace installed at ET during construction, on the grounds that it might prove useful some day. In 1888 the initial open-hearth run using the Thomas process proved so successful that Carnegie at once ordered six more furnaces constructed. "Every day's delay in building . . . is just so much clear profit lost."

Carnegie stood ready to scrap all his Bessemer converters for more modern equipment, despite the hundreds of thousands of dollars invested in them. He knew that the more the furnaces produced the cheaper each ton of steel. That principle dictated the policy of "hard-driving" at blast furnaces and the replacement of old machinery with new provided that the decrease in unit cost paid for the change. At high volumes of steel production, a very small saving per ton justified a very large investment, another example of the tried-and-true formula of "big trains, loaded full, and run fast." British manufacturers, on the other hand, rarely achieved such savings because they regarded the replacement of still serviceable machinery as a wicked waste, a reckless abandon that to English minds rivaled "hard-driving" for managerial irresponsibility. One of them told Carnegie, "We have equipment we have been using for twenty years and it is still serviceable."

"And that," answered Carnegie, "is what is the matter with the British steel trade. Most British equipment is in use twenty years after it should have been scrapped. It is because you keep this used-up machinery that the United States is making you a back number."

Carnegie also understood the implications of economies of scale for production and pricing. He described economy of scale as follows: "Cheapness is in proportion to the scale of production. To make ten tons of steel a day would cost many times as much per ton as to make one-hundred tons. . . . Thus the larger the scale of operation the cheaper the product." He inculcated his staff with these ideas, giving them standing orders to replace obsolete machinery. Bill Jones complied enthusiastically and soon had a renowned dump full of outmoded though not outworn machinery. (Carnegie once ordered Charles Schwab to rip out and rebuild a three-month-old rolling mill when Schwab said he had discovered a better design.)

Since technological improvements often involved successive stages, each more quickly obsolete and more expensive than the preceding, Carnegie's determination to keep pace demanded that he drive most of the profits back into new equipment, rather than pay dividends. The more money the firm made, the more it needed to reinvest. Carnegie never forgot that "We are bound to be followed very soon after we get started." He followed this reinvestment policy fanatically, to the great distress of Phipps, his brother Tom, and the other partners, who itched to spend some of the revenues pouring in. Carnegie owned so large a share that even a small dividend satisfied him, but true to his policy, he concerned himself more with building than spending. Captain Bill, sharing this outlook, declined a partnership in 1879 and asked instead for "a hell of a big salary." Carnegie responded by paying him the same salary as that of the president of the United States, $25,000, which delighted Jones and scandalized Carnegie's antagonists, the "Fathers in Israel." So long as he got his salary, the Captain preferred new machinery to dividends.

Jones himself designed much of the new equipment installed at ET. He concentrated on the mechanical problems of moving and storing material. Until the late 1860s the iron industry consisted of a series of independent operations. Iron ore was dug and smelted into pig iron, which was then hauled to another furnace for reheating and rolling, and so on in a sequence of "small batch" processes. Not only did all the transporting cost money, but the reheating also required time and fuel. Converting the manufacture of steel rails from small batch to continuous flow required vertical integration to get all stages of production under coordinated control, and required development of a whole new arsenal of equipment to reduce interface costs by moving the material from operation to operation swiftly and cheaply. To the latter problem Jones devoted much of his energy.

The Captain's most famous invention, the Jones mixer, greatly reduced costs at the critical point between the blast furnace and the Bessemer converter. Molten iron poured from the furnace directly into the mixer, a huge chest holding two hundred and fifty tons of liquid iron. The chest kept the metal liquid until needed, then poured it into the converter. This eliminated the pig iron stage completely, saving hundreds of thousands of dollars in rehandling and reheating.

The fact that these obstacles, not steel-making operations themselves, limited the maximum output attainable provided another incentive to streamlining the handling of materials. Jones, speaking to British steelmakers in 1881, said, "The output of the American works is governed by the facilities for getting the ingots out of the road. This is the sticking-point just now. Therefore the works that cast their tonnage in the least number of molds have a decided advantage." Jones broke the bottleneck by arranging to cast the ingots from the converter directly onto a train of moving flat cars. Thus rapid movement of material became another hallmark of the Carnegie works, another characteristic that distinguished American mills from their British counterparts. Sidney Gilchrist-Thomas, fascinated by the velocity and volume of steel pouring through Carnegie's establishment, remarked to Alexander Holley (who was guiding him through the plant), "I would like to sit on an ingot for a week and watch that mill operate." Replied Holley, "If you want an ingot cool enough to sit on, you'll have to send to England for it."

The struggle to increase output demanded unrelenting attention because immediately after the removal of one bottleneck, the flow of material rushed forward until it encountered the next constriction. As an older plant's facilities wore out, a firm increasingly had to attack the problems piecemeal, with the added complication of maintaining production while upgrading equipment. A new plant, in contrast, came into being with all the latest improvements ready to go to work at once. The Edgar Thompson Works had this advantage in 1875; in 1881 it passed to the newly opened Homestead works of the Pittsburgh Bessemer Steel Company, located a mile downriver from Braddock.

Homestead possessed the most modern equipment available. Its production soon reached 20 percent of ET's with every sign of increasing. Unfortunately, Homestead soon bogged down in a long series of labor troubles that plagued it intermittently until 1899. After two years of fruitless negotiations with their workers, the Pittsburgh businessmen who owned Homestead asked Carnegie to buy them out. This golden opportunity Carnegie seized immediately, for he recognized the advantages of acquiring at a stroke a completely modern unit. Two years later he converted Homestead to rolling beams and angles in his first major effort at diversifying products to meet the shifting market.

Carnegie's first horizontal integration, Homestead added greatly to his production capacity, but it also added to problems of supply. In the 1870s Carnegie took steps to integrate vertically backward toward raw materials. He bought the Unity and the Larimer Coke works near Connellsville (and brought Cousin Dod over to remodel them and become a partner overnight), the Scotia Ore Mines in Center County, Pennsylvania, and a ferro-manganese mine in Virginia. But these operations provided only a trickle of the growing flood of material Carnegie required.

Above all he needed iron ore and coke. In 1881 he tried to obtain the latter by buying a share of the Henry C. Frick Coke Company. In the process he acquired a share of Mr. Frick. It turned out a fateful bargain.

Henry Frick was a very tough customer. Like Carnegie he had a vision, and he pushed toward it with a vigor, courage, and ruthlessness equal to anything Carnegie could muster. Frick, however, lacked Carnegie's leavening sense of humor, nor had he any counterpart to the Radical conscience that, however much it might flicker at times, always rekindled compassion and remorse in Carnegie's soul eventually. Frick never seemed to regret anything he did. He had that most dangerous of all human qualities, a belief in the rightness of his own actions. All of his actions. At all times.

Frick grew up near Connellsville, Pennsylvania, on a hardscrabble farm. He did not admire his father, who was lazy, pleasant, and poor; rather, he admired his maternal grandfather Abraham Overholt, who was energetic, nasty, and rich. The latter made his fortune distilling Old Overholt whiskey; Henry Frick decided to make his by distilling the local coal into coke. Like Carnegie and Thompson, Frick foresaw steel as king; steel meant coke; coke meant money. Frick aspired to wealth more than anything else. He set out to achieve his goal by gaining control of the coal lands around Connellsville and building coke ovens.

In 1871, to organize the Henry C. Frick Coke Company, he borrowed, begged, coaxed, and cajoled money from friends and neighbors, finally obtaining $10,000 from Judge Thomas Mellon in Pittsburgh. Mellon had the investor's knack for recognizing a timely idea in the hands of the right man to exploit it; in coke and Frick he correctly discerned just such a combination. By 1873 he was selling all the coke he could produce. When the Panic hit, he, like Carnegie fifty miles up the

Monongahela River, expanded rather than contracted his operations. With more of Judge Mellon's money he bought more coal lands at bargain prices. When prosperity returned, coke prices rose steadily, and he and Mellon rejoiced in their foresight. On his thirtieth birthday in 1879, Frick celebrated the fact that he had become a millionaire. By 1880 he had one thousand coke ovens and three thousand acres of land. He wanted still more, and the chance soon came to get it.

In 1881, while on his honeymoon in New York, Frick received an invitation to dine with the Carnegies. Carnegie was Frick's biggest coke customer, but previously the two had had few personal dealings. At dinner Carnegie babbled Celtic charm at the taciturn guest and his new bride. Finally he proposed a toast to the success of the Frick–Carnegie partnership. Although this proposed union came as news to Frick, he agreed readily to its consummation. Frick Coke Company reorganized in 1881 with a capital stock of $2 million. By 1883 Carnegie owned a majority of the shares, although Frick remained president. Carnegie liked what he saw of Frick's executive abilities. They shared a faith in the steel industry's prospects and a dedication to the principle of cost reduction.

As the country, at last recovered from the depression of the 1870s, boomed once again in the 1880s, Carnegie drove his firm on, pushing production up to 10,000, 15,000, 20,000 tons per month, costs down to $40, $30, and $20 per ton, and profits up to a million dollars or more a year. He felt increasingly that Frick should become a partner and take an active role in the steel company's management. In 1886 a series of events underscored the need for a forceful leader at the helm of Carnegie's interests. First, the company's growth had reached the point where it needed a new organizational structure to maximize the advantages of horizontal and vertical integration. Second, Tom Carnegie died, leaving the chairmanship of the company in Harry Phipps's shaky hands. Third, shortly after his mother's death, Carnegie married and began to think seriously of retirement in order to take up full-time the cultural and philanthropic program he had outlined in 1868.

The firm needed an expert organizer. Carnegie set policy, sold products, and watched costs; Bill Jones kept production up at Edgar Thomson, and Schwab did the same at Homestead. Carnegie wanted an executive officer between him and the operational managers, someone attuned to his goals and methods who could effectively coordinate all the efforts in the growing Carnegie properties. Carnegie had repeatedly forced out unsympathetic partners and managers. First went William Coleman, who quarreled with Carnegie over Shinn's management and sold out in 1876. Then David McCandless died in 1878. Carnegie named his brother to succeed McCandless as chairman, an action that ignited a bitter dispute with Shinn, who expected the promotion himself. In his petulance Shinn perpetrated a series of misdemeanors. After demanding an increase in salary to $8,000 per year and getting it, he at once demanded $2,000 more. This affronted Carnegie ("His action after what I have done for him seemed to me ungracious"), who, having made an exception for Bill Jones, shunned high salaries like the plague. He preferred to reward his troops with partnership shares, because he thought profit sharing offered a better incentive.

Soon Carnegie began questioning Shinn's business judgment, in complete contrast to his previous attitude. In 1876 he had written Shinn "I do not know your equal as an Ex[ecutive] officer and I always feel with you at the helm ET is safe. . . . I assure you—there are few nights in which before going to sleep I don't congratulate myself it's our good fortune in having you there." But in 1879 he was losing sleep, complaining to John Scott that Shinn "had gone into a damned gambling operation contracting for 45,000 tons low priced rails without first covering with Pig Iron. I can't trust such speculative people."

Lastly, Shinn committed two unforgivable sins. He learned of a high-grade limestone deposit, and instead of buying it for ET, he formed his own company and bought the limestone beds himself. Then he sold the material to ET, pocketing a large profit. That Carnegie himself had been a virtuoso at such performances while working for the Pennsylvania Railroad did not soften his disapproval—Shinn was stealing his money. Shinn's second offense was still more grievous: he tried to steal Bill Jones. When Carnegie failed to name Shinn chairman, he opened clandestine negotiations for the general managership of Vulcan Iron Company, promising that if he came he could bring Jones. That did it. "Go. Sell out and try another party. We want no drones in the ET if we can help it." Carnegie expelled Shinn, buying out his interest for $200,000 after a dispute over its value.

The incident with Shinn illustrated two of Carnegie's typical tactics. If workers failed to maintain total loyalty, he would mercilessly turn on them. He also held down the book value of his firm by not allowing the capitalization to reflect true assets. The paper value of his partners' shares consequently failed to rise, so that they could not afford to break away. This caused trouble with Shinn, whose share had a nominal worth of only $100,000. He got more only because he threatened to sue, and Carnegie preferred settlement to a public exposure of the firm's real profits and losses.

After Shinn departed, the Edgar Thomson Works, Union Iron, Keystone Bridge, and the minor coke and ore subsidiaries merged into Carnegie Brothers Company, Limited, with a capital of $5 million. Carnegie held 54.4 percent. The other partners in the new firm included Tom Carnegie (chairman of the company), Henry Phipps,

David Stewart, John Scott, Gardner McCandless, John Vandevort, and Cousin Dod Lauder. Carnegie held a small unsubscribed interest in reserve to reward good managers.

Homestead was not incorporated into Carnegie Brothers. Carnegie operated it separately, then merged it and the Lucy Furnaces into Carnegie, Phipps Company, Limited, with John Walker (Phipps's brother-in-law, who came up through the ranks at Lucy Furnace) as chairman. In 1886, then, Carnegie owned controlling interest in two steel firms, each complete with blast furnaces and rolling mills, and in the Frick Coke Company.

Shortly after the organization of Carnegie, Phipps Company, Tom Carnegie died. Tom had neither learned to share his brother's empire-building fervor nor to cut himself loose altogether. He had lived in Andy's shadow since childhood, and remained an unhappy satellite all his life. When a mutual friend told Tom the story of Andy's jubilant announcement in 1863, "I'm rich; I'm rich!" Tom wryly remarked, "Yes, and we have never been so rich since."

Tom had mostly spent his adult life "minding the store" while Andy basked in the spotlight. In 1865, for example, as soon as he put together Union Mills, Andy went to Europe, leaving Tom to guide the firm through its initial struggles. In 1878 he sailed around the world, instructing Tom and Phipps to watch Shinn. After Shinn's dismissal, Tom became chairman. In each capacity he suffered as a sitting target for Andy's abuse. Andrew dealt with Tom as he did with his other supervisors, feeding him caustic billingsgate, outrageous demands, and emotional pep talks, spiced with occasional bursts of outlandish flattery, such as this specimen written from Adelsburg, Austria:

> The more I feel myself drinking in enjoyment, the deeper is my appreciation of your devoted self-denial and the oftener I resolve that you shall have the opportunity to enjoy what I am now doing. . . . It is a heavy load for a youngster to carry, but if you succeed it will be a lasting benefit to you.

In fact, it destroyed him finally, for although Tom had the talent for his responsibilities—a "sagacious business man" Captain Bill called him—he never developed a passion for them. In the early 1880s he became a heavy drinker, and in October 1886 the habit killed him. He died a month before his mother.

After Tom's death, Carnegie temporarily appointed Phipps general manager of Carnegie Brothers and made Frick a partner by selling him a 2 percent interest for $184,000. In time-honored fashion the share cost Frick nothing: retained dividends soon paid for it. Using the same method, Frick acquired an 11 percent interest in January 1889. Carnegie then named him chairman of the company. "Take good care of that head of yours," he wrote Frick. "It is wanted. Again, expressing my thankfulness that I have found THE MAN, I am always yours, A. C."

Relief in finding "the man" stemmed not only from business but also from personal considerations. Carnegie's outside activities had always taken up much of his time. By putting Frick in charge of operations, he freed himself to devote even more time to these interests. Having abandoned his career as bond salesman in 1873, he continued overseas travels for pleasure and edification. In 1878, while on a tour around the world, he found evidence for Darwinism on every hand. Evolution, he concluded, was a universal not an Anglo-Saxon phenomenon.

> The Japanese, Chinese, Cingalese, Indians, Egyptians, all have been made our friends. . . . Wherever we have been, one story met us. Everywhere there is progress, not only material but intellectual progress as well, and rapid progress too. . . . The law of evolution—the higher from the lower—is not discredited by a voyage round the world.

Following the excursion, Carnegie made a coach trip through England and Scotland that culminated in the triumphal return to Dunfermline. In 1884 he repeated the journey in England accompanied by the English poets Edwin and Matthew Arnold, and the novelist William Black, who, wearied by Carnegie's ceaseless tirades about the failings of the old country and the virtues of the new, dubbed him "The Star Spangled Scotchman." He wryly noted:

> We had such a discourse on the freedom and purity and incorruptibility of the United States . . . that we longed . . . to fly away and be at rest in that happy land. Why should we be lingering here in slavery? . . . As we listened the land of promise grew more and more fair, more and more dismal and desperate became the results of a monarchial system of government. We couldn't see any of them, it is true; for the Wiltshire hawthorne bushes are thick, and around us were only pleasant meadows and rippling streams, but they were there somewhere; and we wondered that the birds, in such a condition of affairs could sing so carelessly.

Carnegie's peregrinations about the countryside in the company of intellectuals show the success of his program of "making the acquaintance of literary men" laid down in 1868. Like so many of his countrymen, Carnegie coupled his professed abhorrence of English society, manners, snobbishness, and educational institutions with a manifest veneration for its most accomplished products. Consequently, when he began collecting philosophers and literati, he concentrated largely on English "specimens"— the Arnolds, Herbert Spencer, William E. Gladstone.

The Arnolds and Spencer he induced to come to the United States on lecture tours. When they arrived he overwhelmed them with hospitality. Pittsburgh's smoke and grime, which Carnegie pointed out as epitomizing the evolutionary process, inspired Spencer's comment: "Six months residence here would justify suicide." Edwin Arnold, battered by the enthusiasm of his host, told his doctor that he had to get out of America or he would die;

he canceled his lecture tour and escaped to the peace and quiet of Japan.

Despite these mishaps, Carnegie built genuine friendships with many intellectuals. Spencer called him "my best American friend." Matthew Arnold, whom Carnegie called "the most charming man I ever knew," respected him and introduced him in 1883 to John Morley, editor of the *Fortnightly Review* and the *Pall Mall Gazette* and cabinet minister under Gladstone. Through Morley he met Gladstone, Joseph Chamberlin, and other Liberal Party potentates with whom he later corresponded regularly, forming friendships among his industrialist contemporaries. His wealth opened this world to him, but once inside he gave and received a genuine respect for intellectual rather than material achievements. It is hard to imagine Jay Gould or Cornelius Vanderbilt strolling comfortably in Gladstone's garden at Hawardon, discussing the merits of Irish Home Rule. Carnegie derived deep satisfaction from these friendships. They added to his life a dimension that he had craved since boyhood, and they helped provide "that life . . . most elevating in its character" to balance those "thoughts wholly upon the way to make more money in the shortest time," which he had feared in 1868 "must degrade me beyond hope of permanent recovery."

An even greater uplift came from his marriage. In 1880 Carnegie met Louise Whitfield, the daughter of a New York merchant. Carnegie was forty-five years old and five-feet-three; Louise twenty-three and five-feet-six. No matter. They fell in love and would have married sooner but Margaret Carnegie, who wanted no rival for her son's attentions, demanded that her son remain unmarried. Margaret, whom Louise later described as the most unpleasant person she had ever known, remained implacably hostile to the idea of marriage for her son. Andrew, who feared no rival in the no-holds-barred world of late-nineteenth-century American industry, could not defy his mother, and abided by her wishes. A tempestuous courtship resulted, punctuated with hope, despair, and broken engagements. He often treated Louise shabbily, as galloping around the world, leaving her alone and miserable at home to read his cheerful travelogues from Paris and Rome. Few women would have endured it, but she loved him, and she waited. Finally in 1886 the commitment came: "Louise I am now wholly yours—all gone but you. . . . I live in you now. . . . Till death, Louise, yours alone."

They married on April 22, 1887; it proved a happy match. Carnegie called Louise "the peacemaker" and rejoiced in her support of the goal he now set himself, giving away his fortune so constructively that he could justify having amassed it in the first place.

In 1889 Carnegie published an article titled "Wealth" (more commonly known as "The Gospel of Wealth," the title used in England) in the *North American Review*. It was not Carnegie's first literary publication. He had previously published *Round the World* (1878), *An American Four in Hand in Britain* (1883), and *Triumphant Democracy* (1886). The first two were travelogues, the third a statistical exposition of his patriotic theme which purported to show that rising production proved the virtues of democracy. "Wealth," however, took another tack entirely. It elaborated on his earlier reflections that he had a personal responsibility to "spend the surplus . . . for benevolent purposes." In it Carnegie remarked publicly (as he had already told Gladstone privately) that a man who died rich died disgraced. The rich man had a duty to dispose of his wealth by supporting useful institutions, of which he listed seven: universities, libraries, hospitals, parks, meeting and concert halls, swimming pools, and church buildings. In these benefactions the rich fulfilled the only function that justified their existence—accumulating wealth for the uplift of the general populace. Carnegie had already embarked on his philanthropic career. In 1873 he had given Dunfermline a swimming pool; in 1881, a library. He had also built a library in Braddock, donated an organ to the Swedenborgian church (his father's) in Allegheny, and given $6,000 to the University of Western Pennsylvania (now the University of Pittsburgh). But these efforts only symbolized the possibilities. In 1889 he declared his intention to move forward toward the goal of giving away his fortune. To doubters, and there were many, he replied simply, "Wait and see." He was fifty-four years old and knew he must act soon. But first he had the business to take care of. In 1883 Carnegie had thought of selling out. Now in 1889 he made another effort to find a buyer, but a suitable customer failed to materialize. As soon as Frick took control of the firm, his stewardship produced such impressive results that Carnegie lost his urgency to sell. Profits rose from $2 million in 1888 to $3.5 million in 1889 and $5.4 million in 1890.

With Frick at the helm, Carnegie looked to the future with confidence. He had a net worth of $30 million and an income of $2 million a year. He enjoyed recognition as one of the most famous industrialists in the world. He had a secure, happy marriage, a growing circle of friends, and a blueprint for the rest of his life.

Unfortunately, in the words of his favorite poet, Robert Burns, "The best laid schemes . . . gang aft a-gley," for while Carnegie perfected his firm and found the man to run it, the currents of discontent that had stirred among Americans in the 1870s coalesced in the 1880s, into gale force winds bearing demands for change. Seeking a greater share in the profits flowing from their labor, workers organized unions such as the Knights of Labor, which tried to organize all the workers in vast new industries, and the American Federation of Labor (AF of L), which tried to protect the traditional wages and privileges enjoyed by skilled tradesmen. Violent strikes and confrontations ensued, as labor grappled for a strategy to match the power of new industrial combinations.

In politics, the People's Party (Populists) built a coalition of farmers, miners, and workers that demanded government intervention to restore what they perceived as the betrayed promises of America, and to rein in the abuses of industrial giants that had waxed so mighty that nothing short of the full force of government could restrain them. Certainly the Carnegie Company exemplified the mighty industrial firm on the march, trampling those in its way.

Carnegie had observed the power of labor's wrath in 1877, when the Pennsylvania's workers had burned the railroad's buildings and equipment to the ground; moreover, his colleagues had warned him that his own turn might someday come. But Carnegie thought that Social Darwinism justified the accumulators of wealth, provided they ultimately channeled it into beneficent causes; moreover, his own deft touch with workers—polished on the railroad—and Captain Bill Jones's ability to restrain Carnegie's occasional urge to squeeze his workers harder than usual and even to win for them a concession now and then had largely maintained labor peace in his various enterprises. The 1890s, however, shattered this equilibrium. American labor, driven to desperation by yet another industrial recession that began in 1893, confronted business firms determined to hold their ground. When troubles came to Carnegie Steel, the workers encountered not the image-conscious Carnegie, proud of his reputation as a friend of the working man, but the hard case Henry Frick, determined to prevail at all costs. For Carnegie, the costs exceeded his worst fears.

The Homestead riot, 1892: Pinkerton men leaving the barges after the surrender

IX

Triumph and Tragedy

In the decade after Henry Frick's appointment as chairman of the Carnegie Company, the firm weathered the most arduous passage of its history. The tragedy of the Homestead strike of 1892 was followed by the depression of 1893, which lasted four years. The return of prosperity brought a powerful new array of business competitors to the battle for supremacy. Although the struggle for survival distracted him from other projects dear to his heart, Carnegie the businessman triumphed in the end: Carnegie Steel became a superb industrial unit, with an efficiency unmatched in the world; however, Carnegie the public figure never recovered the reputation lost in the Homestead strike.

Frick's first achievement as chairman exceeded Carnegie's highest expectations. Topping Carnegie's Homestead coup, Frick bought the beleaguered Duquesne Steel Works, five miles below Homestead on the Monongahela, at the time the most modern steel mill in the world. Once again the Carnegie Company made up all lost scientific ground and technical ground at a stroke. Despite its sophisticated technology, Duquesne had problems similar to Homestead's. Labor strife and capital shortages had beset the mill since its opening in 1889. Carnegie himself damaged Duquesne's reputation by spreading a rumor that its rails would not have "homogeneity" due to their new manufacturing process. Worse than false, the charge had no meaning. Duquesne got off to a bad start, nevertheless, because prospective customers worried about the "defect" even though they had no idea what it was.

In the fall of 1889 Frick offered Duquesne's owners $600,000 for the plant. They declined. In the summer of 1890 he offered $1 million in bonds; they accepted. Before the bonds matured in five years, the plant's operations had earned the principal and interest five times over. Duquesne's efficiency stemmed from reductions in movement of materials. Its designers sought to save expenses by "direct rolling." Ingots came out of their molds and went immediately into the rollers without being reheated. This was the mysterious innovation that Carnegie had accused of destroying homogeneity. What it actually destroyed, of course, was his cost advantage. Once Carnegie took over Duquesne, no further mention of homogeneity surfaced; moreover, the firm installed forthwith the direct rolling process at ET and Homestead. In each of the Carnegie plants, the raw material emerged as finished product without undergoing any heating other than that in the operations of smelting and refining. This took a great stride toward the ultimate goal of continuous flow steel production. The savings in fuel and labor contributed significantly to the declining cost of rails and beams.

Once he had absorbed Duquesne, Frick streamlined the company. On July 1, 1892, Carnegie Steel Company, Limited took over all assets of Carnegie Brothers and of Carnegie Phipps. The new firm had a nominal capital of $25 million (though its real worth far exceeded that figure), of which Carnegie owned 55 percent, Frick and Phipps 11 percent each, and nineteen other partners 1 percent each. The company held 4 percent in reserve to reward its successful "racehorses." The new firm owned three complete steel mills—Edgar Thomson, Homestead, and Duquesne—plus Keystone Bridge, Union Iron, Lucy Furnaces, and sundry supportive operations. Of the original nine partners, only Carnegie and Phipps remained. Frick had extensive plans involving consolidation and vertical integration, but before he could launch them, the Homestead strike broke out.

Before this strike in 1892, Carnegie's companies had had relatively few labor problems. Because Carnegie had kept his mills running full, his workers had enjoyed steady employment. Moreover, his companies had not followed anti-union policies. At Edgar Thomson, Union Iron, and Keystone Bridge the company had signed a number of contracts with the United Sons of Vulcan and its successor, the Amalgamated Association of Iron and Steel Workers. Captain Bill Jones's charismatic leadership and intelligent handling of labor problems also kept troubles to a minimum.

Carnegie, who watched labor costs as closely as he watched every other expenditure, constantly pressed Jones to cut wages. Captain Bill had his own ideas. In 1878 he told Carnegie to "leave good enough alone. Don't think of any further reductions. Our men are working hard and faithfully, believing that the hard pan has been reached. . . . Mark what I tell you. Our labor is the cheapest in the country. Our men have 'Esprit de Corps.'" Jones's fundamental doctrine was: "Low wages does not always imply cheap labor. Good wages and good workmen I know to be cheap labor." The captain also argued that "The men should be made to feel that the company are interested in their welfare. Make the works a pleasant place for them."

This last was a tall order. No one ever mistook a steel mill for a picnic ground even during the best of times, and Jones's men worked a twelve-hour day seven days a week. (The weekend shift required that the Sunday day shift work twenty-four consecutive hours. The men liked it, the company claimed, because it gave them every other Sunday off.) Nevertheless, Jones felt that he could regulate his men's labors so as to keep up morale:

> I have always found it best to treat men well, and I find that my men are anxious to return my good will by working steadily and honestly, and instead of dodging are anxious to show me what a good day's work they have done. All haughty and disdainful treatment of men has a very decided and bad effect upon them.

Jones had sophisticated theories about the makeup of his crews:

> We must be careful what class of men we collect. . . . We must steer clear as far as we can of Englishmen who are great sticklers for high wages, small production and strikes. My experience has shown that Germans and Irish, Swedes and what I denominate "Buckwheats"—young American country boys, judiciously mixed, make the most effective and tractable force you can find. Scotsmen do very well, are honest and faithful. Welsh can be used in limited numbers. But mark me, Englishmen have been the worst class of men I have had anything to do with; and this is [also] the opinion of Mr. Holley, George and John Fritz.

The Captain's success in keeping his crews happy partly resulted from his policy of keeping them "judiciously mixed." Left to themselves, the men would separate into antipathetic ethnic groups; and these divisions led to disputes over job jurisdictions, promotions, and hiring. Such polarization agitated the already constant turmoil in the anthracite coal mines around Jones's home. It also had much to do with the labor troubles encountered by the original Homestead owners. There the Welsh controlled the rail mill and the Irish, the converting works. Other nationalities also carved out little fiefdoms; these domains often struck sparks when they overlapped. Lost production resulted. Jones never let that kind of trouble get started. Instead, his ethnically mixed crews engaged in rivalries of production, which vastly benefited the company. The blast furnace crews, for example, labored mightily to achieve the highest output for the week to win the symbol of supremacy, a steel broom which, when displayed high on the furnace's stack, proclaimed to Pittsburgh who the mightiest men in town were. By encouraging such competition Jones made testosterone a potent ingredient in steelmaking, and increased productivity without adding a cent to the wage bill.

Captain Bill even persuaded Carnegie to put his mills on three eight-hour shifts instead of two twelve-hour ones. They ran that way for two years, in hopes that competitors would follow suit. Carnegie enjoyed appearing as an enlightened pioneer in labor policies. The Captain brought out this benevolent side of him and acted as a buffer against the excesses of his cost mania. Unfortunately, Jones died in a blast furnace explosion at ET in September 1889. Thereafter any amelioration of the harsh labor practices of the era depended solely on Carnegie's desire to seem the working man's friend.

Carnegie had published his guidelines for labor practices in two 1886 *Forum* articles, "An Employer's View of the Labor Question" and "Results of the Labor Struggle." Carried away by his own rhetoric, Carnegie painted himself into a corner. The first article argued that the refusal of American employers to recognize labor unions led to unnecessary bitterness. Citing the decision of Chief Justice Lemuel Shaw of Massachusetts forty-five years earlier,

Carnegie defended "the right of the working men to combine and to form trades unions" as "no less sacred than the right of the manufacturer to enter into associations . . . with his fellows." He then proposed a sliding scale that would tie workers' wages to employers' prices.

This piece appeared just in time for a general railroad strike followed by the Haymarket Riots; Carnegie, confident of the inherent conservatism of American workers, felt the need to reassure the public that red revolution did not impend. The workers, Carnegie argued, resorted to violence only when employers brought in strikebreakers. Thus his second article asked that "the public give due consideration to the terrible temptation to which the working man on strike is sometimes subjected. To expect that one dependent on his daily wage for the necessaries of life will stand peaceably and see a new man employed in his stead is to expect too much." Except for railroads and other public service agencies, industries that were struck should not hire scab labor; they should simply shut down and "await the result." Scab labor not only caused trouble but also did poor work. "Neither the best men as men, nor the best men as workers, are thus to be obtained. There is an unwritten law among the best workmen: Thou shalt not take thy neighbor's job." This extraordinary statement had no parallel in public utterances by other major American industrialists of the time. Carnegie's continual need to reconcile his role as wealthy employer with his Radical conscience convinced him that good treatment of workers made for good business. (Captain Bill, of course, had told him so repeatedly.)

Carnegie basked in the praise that subsequently flowed in from labor leaders everywhere. The Brotherhood of Locomotive Engineers named a lodge after him, an honor he gratefully acknowledged. He should have realized, however, that he set a collision course with Frick, from whom he could expect no approval.

Frick's attitudes toward the workers could only euphemistically be described as "haughty and disdainful." Nor did he subscribe to Carnegie's unwritten law. He believed in the written laws that stated he could do with his property as he liked—bring anyone on it, keep anyone off it, and otherwise use and benefit from it in any legal way he chose. This position soon brought him into conflict with Carnegie, for labor wasted no time in testing Andy's sincerity, and the first test involved the Frick Coke Company.

In the spring of 1887 the workers in the coal mines and coke plants of the Connellsville region struck. Frick favored a hard line and made an agreement with his fellow coke manufacturers to yield no ground to the strikers and to bring in strikebreakers to resume production. The coal miners, a hard-bitten lot for whom death and violence were routine, had ready access to dynamite and knew how to use it to blow mines up as well as knock coal down. Both sides entrenched themselves for a struggle.

Others, including Henry Phipps, chairman of Carnegie Brothers, and John Walker, chairman of Carnegie Phipps, fretted, impatient for a settlement. Both men had mills running full blast and large back orders; neither could tolerate the threatened loss of profits. Phipps and Walker cabled Carnegie, who was honeymooning on the Isle of Wight. Carnegie fired off a peremptory ukase ordering Frick to settle on the strikers' terms.

Frick had to obey; he was hoist with his own petard, because Carnegie, as majority stockholder in Frick Coke, based his authority on the very laws of property so dear to Frick's soul. Nonetheless, he felt betrayed and foolish, for he who had urged his colleagues to take a rigid stand now became the first to abandon it. He also believed that Carnegie's willingness to surrender to the strikers in no small degree reflected the fact that the name on the company door was Frick's, not Carnegie's. Incensed, Frick threatened to resign, stating his objection "to so manifest a prostitution of the Coke Company's interests in your determination to promote your steel interests."

Carnegie might well have taken warning from this outburst; however, he apparently respected Frick's vigorous defense of his own interest and felt that when Frick became a partner in Carnegie Steel he would transfer this fierce dedication to his new domain. In any case, he, Phipps, Lauder, and others placated their churlish partner and eventually enticed him back to the fold.

The next test of Carnegie's labor attitudes came in the winter of 1887–1888. Carnegie had decided to terminate the eight-hour experiment at Edgar Thomson and to inaugurate a sliding scale that tied wages to steel prices. He posted a notice to this effect for January 1, 1888. ET's workers put down their tools and went home. Carnegie withdrew to his fortifications—he shut down the works and retired to his home in New York.

A workers' committee arrived to negotiate. Turning on the charm, Carnegie told them amusing stories about the steel business, gave them copies of his *Forum* articles, introduced them to the Prime Minister of Siam who had dropped by for tea (what the parties to that pleasantry thought of each other is a joy to contemplate), and—refused to budge an inch. No one would work except on his terms, but no one would work without a settlement either: "We will never try to fill our works with new men . . . we could never get such good men as you are. It is the scallawags who are idle and looking for work when there is a strike. . . . No one will ever have your places here. We like you too much." There matters rested for four months. At first the firm hardly suffered, because the rail market declined coincidentally. When orders did come in, Carnegie rejected them. Confronted again by a workers' committee in New York, Carnegie gave them lunch and a tour of Central Park, but no concessions.

Finally, after a shutdown of nearly five months, Carnegie appeared at a mass meeting of ET's employees. The tense atmosphere frightened Phipps and Lauder, but Carnegie, who never feared his workers ("There can never be any hopeless troubles . . . as long as they call me 'Andy'"), clambered up on the platform and asked for individual grievances. One worker rose. "Mr. Carnegie, you take my job—" He got no farther. "Mr. Carnegie takes no man's job," Andy interjected. The tension broke; the battle was won. The men voted to go back to work. Carnegie had come out victorious.

His faith in his program's efficacy strengthened considerably the following year when one of his managers abandoned it with unhappy results. In 1889 the firm's contract with the Amalgamated Association at Homestead expired. In April Carnegie instructed his minions to institute a sliding scale and, if that provoked a strike, to deal with it as he had at ET. He then sailed off to Scotland for his annual six months' retreat. On July 1 the strike began. W. L. Abbott, in his first year as president of Carnegie, Phipps Company, lacked his boss's tenacity; he sent for strikebreakers. Soon a trainload arrived, escorted by the sheriff and one hundred and twenty-five deputies. This small detachment proved no match for the two thousand angry strikers and their families, who routed the interlopers with a shower of spit, brickbats, and obscenities.

When the news of this engagement reached Braddock, ET's men considered joining in a sympathy strike. In anticipation of this development Carnegie had left Bill Jones elaborate instructions about what he should say to keep his workers' shoulders to the wheel. How well Jones might have performed his dummy's role in Carnegie's ventriloquist act we will never know, for Abbott lost his nerve, called in the Amalgamated's leaders, and signed a new three-year contract. The union accepted the sliding scale, and the company recognized the union as the exclusive bargaining agent for Homestead. This agreement Carnegie regarded as an abject submission to violence. "The great objection to the compromise," he wrote Abbott, was "that it was made under intimidation—our men in other works now know that we will 'confer' with law breakers." A better policy would have dictated "a curt refusal to have anything to do with these men. [This] would have brought matters right." He reiterated his policy: "Whenever we are compelled to make a stand we shall have to shut down and wait as at ET until part of the men vote to work."

The Homestead strike of 1892 took place against this backdrop. When the contract came up for renewal, Abbott had long since gone the way of those partners who turned out to be carthorses rather than racehorses. The taciturn Mr. Frick now occupied the seat of power. The Amalgamated Association, however, approached the confrontation confident that as long as Carnegie owned the mills, he would restrain Frick. They erred. Carnegie and Frick had concurred on a two-point negotiation program, and although they differed on how best to secure the men's acceptance of it, Carnegie did not limit Frick's discretionary powers. On the contrary, Carnegie carefully left his manager's hands free.

The first item on the Carnegie–Frick agenda was a reduction of the minimum on the sliding scale which had a lower but not an upper limit. At Homestead, wages were tied to the price of steel billets; wages rose if prices did. The reverse applied, however, only until billets dropped to $25 per ton. At that point wages froze, no matter how low the price went. The company wanted to reduce the minimum to $22. The second part of the program was worse from the workers' standpoint. Carnegie and Frick wanted to eliminate the union as bargaining agent. Carnegie wanted simply to proclaim the firm's plants as henceforth nonunion. Frick had more devious methods in mind.

In 1892 Carnegie went to Scotland shortly before the contract expired, thus removing himself from the scene of the battle just as he had in 1889. Before leaving, he urged his usual negotiating program on Frick:

> My idea . . . is always to shut down and suffer. Let them decide by vote when they decide to go to work. Say kindly "All right, gentlemen, let's hear from you; no quarrel, not the least in the world. Until a majority vote (secret ballot) to go to work, have a good time; when a majority vote to start, start it is."

Whatever course Carnegie thought events would take, he did not order Frick to follow his program as such. He wrote Frick from England that he really did "not believe it will be much of a struggle. We all approve of anything you do, not stopping short of . . . a contest. We are with you to the end. . . . Your reputation will shorten [the] struggle."

Frick gloried in his reputation as the strongest antilabor man in business. He preferred to fight and had told Carnegie so. Carnegie gave Frick a blank check and left England for Scotland. Significantly, he departed from his custom of inviting all his friends to drop in. Instead, he went into seclusion, giving his address only to a trusted few. Apparently his partners feared that if the press or his workers reached Carnegie, his resolve might weaken and he might once again intervene. Phipps and Lauder in particular wanted to avoid involving Carnegie because they knew Frick would resign as he had before when Carnegie meddled. Quite simply they wanted Frick in charge of Carnegie Steel because he seemed likely to make a lot of money for them by holding down wages. If Carnegie returned, his occasional preference for adulation rather than money might prompt an expensive settlement.

Carnegie accepted the "exile" because he knew his own weakness—that indeed if reached by press or workers he might well give in, and because he felt trapped between his determination to gain absolute control over wage costs on the one hand, and his delight in his reputation as the working man's friend. So he pulled the covers over his head to shut out the sounds of conflict, hoping that when he pulled them off, all would be well, his image preserved by his absence, and blame (if any) attached to Frick. From Scotland he wrote Frick "Of course you will win, and win easier than you suppose, owing to the present condition of the market."

Frick took no chances. He meant to take the offensive. He erected a massive stockade around the works, complete with watchtowers, rifle slits, and barbed wire. Then he ordered the Pinkerton detective agency to assemble three hundred of their finest. To force an all-out struggle, Frick presented the Amalgamated's officers with demands he knew they would have to reject. He planned to have the Pinkertons take over the works and then reopen with nonunion help—with the old employees if they would work, with scabs if they would not.

On July 1 the strike began. Frick ordered the Pinkertons to arrive on July 6, barging down the river at night, in absolute secrecy. He hoped to smuggle them into the plant and present the strikers with a *fait accompli* at sunrise. The workers foiled the plan by spotting the barges passing through Pittsburgh and sending word ahead. The alarm sounded; the population of Homestead rushed to the river bank and launched a ferocious though inept assault.

The battle lasted all day as the strikers kept the Pinkertons pinned down on the barges and tried to kill every last one of them. That they failed testified only to their lack of skill, not to lack of desire. They charged the town's courthouse cannon with dynamite; it blew up. They poured oil on the river and set fire to it; the wind blew it the wrong way. They threw a lighted stick of dynamite onto a barge; it rolled into a bucket of water. They loaded a flatcar with blazing combustibles and pushed it down the track toward the barges; it derailed.

Finally, in the late afternoon a truce was negotiated. The Pinkertons dropped their guns, and the strikers promised them safe conduct out of town. Unfortunately the promise could not be kept. The fury of the bystanders exceeded even that of the combatants; the Pinkertons had to run the gauntlet of the howling mob. When the battle ended, four guards had died and all the others had sustained injuries.

The rest of the tragedy ran its course quickly. The governor sent eight thousand troops who occupied the plant. Frick received knife and bullet wounds from a would-be assassin. Although the assailant had no connection with the union, his bullet, as one of the Amalgamated's officers said, "went straight through the heart of the Homestead Strike." Frick, though wounded, remained in control and reopened the plant. Satisfied with the outcome and the strategy used to obtain it, he told Carnegie later, "If we had adopted the policy of sitting down and waiting we would have still been sitting, waiting . . . the fight would yet have to be made and then we would . . . be accused of trying to starve our men into submission." This attitude Frick adhered to forever.

Carnegie's emotions, on the other hand, had run the gamut from determination to panic to despair as he realized the implications of the battle for his cherished reputation. On the day following the clash, he cabled Frick: "All anxiety gone since you stand firm. Never employ one of these rioters. Let grass grow over the works. . . . Use your discretion about terms and starting. George Lauder, Henry Phipps, Jr. Andrew Carnegie solid. H. C. Frick forever."

But Carnegie began to pivot as the wind blew foul. He wrote Lauder:

> Matters at home *bad*—such a fiasco trying to send guards by boat and then leaving space between River & fences for the men to get opposite the landing. . . . We must keep quiet and

do all we can to support Frick and those at the Seat of War. I have been besieged by interviewing cables from N. York but have not said a word. Silence is best.

And Carnegie maintained silence publicly. True to his code, he supported Frick's conduct in his public remarks. The public, however, rightly blamed Carnegie, the owner. On both sides of the Atlantic the newspapers attacked him. In England the *St. James Gazette* said, "Mr. Andrew Carnegie has preached to us upon 'Triumphant Democracy,' he has lectured us upon the rights and duties of wealth. . . . It is indeed a wholesome piece of satire." The *St. Louis Post-Dispatch* made the most savage thrust:

Count no man happy until he is dead. Three months ago Andrew Carnegie was a man to be envied. Today he is an object of mingled pity and contempt. In the estimation of nine-tenths of the thinking people on both sides of the ocean he has not only given the lie to all his antecedents, but confessed himself a moral coward. One would naturally suppose that if he had a grain of consistency, not to say decency, in his composition, he would favor rather than oppose the organization of trades-unions among his own working people at Homestead. One would naturally suppose that if he had a grain of manhood, not to say courage, in his composition, he would at least have been willing to face the consequences of his inconsistency. But what does Carnegie do? Runs off to Scotland out of harm's way to await the issue of the battle he was too pusillanimous to share. A single word from him might have saved the bloodshed—but the word was never spoken. Nor has he, from that bloody day until this, said anything except that he had "implicit confidence in the managers of the mills." The correspondent who finally obtained this valuable information expresses the opinion that "Mr. Carnegie has no intention of returning to America at present." He might have added that America can well spare Mr. Carnegie. Ten thousand "Carnegie Public Libraries" would not compensate the country for the direct and indirect evils resulting from the Homestead lockout. Say what you will of Frick, he is a brave man. Say what you will of Carnegie, he is a coward. And gods and men hate cowards.

Despite his public support for Frick, Carnegie privately felt that Frick's obduracy had stupidly twisted a crisis into a disaster, and that he, Carnegie, had to undergo these scathing attacks because Frick had not carried out his policy. He wrote Gladstone that Frick had blundered by trying "to run the Homestead Works with new men. [That was] a test to which working men should not [have been] subjected. It [was] expecting too much of poor men to stand idly by and see their work taken by others." Carnegie attempted to exculpate himself: "The pain I suffer increases daily. The Works are not worth one drop of human blood. I wish they had sunk." In his heart, of course, he knew where the fault lay. His *Autobiography* contains a lengthy, anecdote-filled account of his long, happy relations with workers. He put some of the strike leaders on his private pension list (although some refused him), and one of his first philanthropies after retirement endowed a relief fund for Homestead employees. Late in life he wrote, "No pangs remain of any wound received in my business career save that of Homestead. . . . I was the controlling owner. That was sufficient to make my name a by-word for years."

Carnegie did not need newspaper editorials to remind him what a mockery the Homestead bloodshed had made of *Triumphant Democracy,* "The Gospel of Wealth," and his prattlings about the dignity of work and the rights of the worker. His chagrin subsequently released enormous energy and determination. He had considered retirement; now he put it aside. He had relinquished control; now he reasserted it more vigorously than ever. He never again trusted Frick. As he guided his firm over the hurdles of the 1890s, he kept Frick under tight rein.

The confrontation at Homestead had, however, resulted from much more than Frick's obsessions, Carnegie's cowardice, and the Homestead workers' desperate resort to violence. By the 1890s, the incompatible imperatives of management's drive to maintain profits by controlling wages had collided with workers' need for job security and a living wage. This conflict over equitable distribution of business income between capital and labor obscured an even more desperate struggle over control of the workplace, including issues such as hiring and firing, the processes used, and the pace of work. All these things skilled workers had controlled, empowered by their mastery of the arts of production; all these things management now determined to control, substituting machine tools for human skills, science and technology-based production systems for the traditional craftsman's art, and matching the work pace to the capacity of the machine rather than to workers' traditions.

This unequal struggle the workers had not won against the railroads in the 1870s, nor against International Harvester in the 1880s. It could not win in the 1890s, not against Frick, nor as subsequent events showed, not against George Pullman or other industrial titans in late-nineteenth- and early-twentieth-century America. The public and the courts, like Frick, privileged the rights of property over any workers' claims for equity. Against the ferocious opposition of employers, backed by the courts, the police, militia, and federal troops, labor could field no organization powerful enough to hold its own against business until the Wagner Act (labor's "Magna Carta") of 1935 legitimized industrial unions such as the United Steel Workers.

Carnegie was fifty-seven at the time of the Homestead strike. In the ensuing years he gave the virtuoso performance of his life, summoning all his knowledge and skills to survive the recession and to vanquish his rivals. He knew he could not erase the memory of Homestead, but he could try to bury it under new achievements. All his life he had assuaged his hungers, griefs, and wounds by doing, working, achieving. He had suffered a massive setback; fortunately, he had massive challenges to confront.

Henry Clay Frick

X

Carnegie Challenges the World

Carnegie Steel's first major problem after Homestead was the depression that began in 1893. Carnegie had sensed that American manufacturing as a whole suffered from excess capacity; he knew full well that the steel industry in particular did. Eight of the thirteen major rail mills established in his time had failed; he had taken over two of them. The worst lay ahead, as he advised his partners: "The demand will just fall short of the capacity to produce, therefore a struggle must ensue among producers for orders. . . . The sooner you scoop the market the better." In time of recession, "It has never failed that the lowest price given has proved to be a high price at time of delivery on a falling market. When you want to capture a falling stone, it won't do to follow it. You must cut under it, and so it is with a falling market." A policy of aggressive price cutting continues to yield profits if backed with equally aggressive attention to costs; the old formulas must be applied with renewed vigor: the mills must run full with continually updated equipment; profits must go to machinery, not to dividends. Backward integration must ensure cheap, dependable sources of raw material; transportation costs must be beaten down to a minimum. The firm must also energetically promote campaigns to update and expand the sales organization, find new markets, and develop new products.

Implementing these ambitious policies required enthusiastic support from associates. Carnegie drove them harder than ever before—they had to produce or get out. To follow their work more closely, he ordered extensive minutes compiled from board meetings so "that the votes of each member . . . shall be recorded," along with "every reason or explanation." Then anyone "looking over the minutes would be able to judge of the judgment displayed by the voter, which of course would affect his standing with his colleagues."

Under such pressure, the staff suffered high attrition rates. One of the first displaced was Frick. In December 1894 he submitted another of his many resignations, this time in pique at Carnegie's intention to add a coke firm, W. J. Rainey Company, to Frick Coke and change the business's name to Frick-Rainey Coke Company. Solicitously Carnegie told Frick he suffered from overwork: "You are not well my friend. . . . Go to Egypt . . . take the cure." At one point Frick threateningly replied that unless Carnegie stopped referring to his supposed ill health, "I will take such measures as will convince you that I am fully able to take care of myself." After increasingly acrimonious exchanges Carnegie finally wrote:

> This is not the first time you have resigned. . . . Well you resign again and I have tried my best to be your friend again. It is simply ridiculous my dear Mr. Frick, that any full grown man is not to make the acquaintance of Mr. Rainey, or anybody else, without your august permission—really laughable. . . . You are determined to resign. All right.

So ended Frick's career as chief operating executive of Carnegie Steel. He asked Carnegie to name him chairman of the board, an honorary position, to save him from public embarrassment. Carnegie agreed, although he subsequently regretted it. Frick continued as head of the coke company and as a partner in Carnegie Steel. His 11 percent interest fell to 6 percent, the balance going to his successor J. G. Leishman. Leishman himself soon proved unsatisfactory. In 1897 Carnegie caught him speculating in pig iron and ore. He had thereby committed the sins of speculation and disloyalty. "You have not treated me fairly as your partner," he told Leishman. "You . . . deluded me. You deceived your partner and friend." Carnegie replaced Leishman with Schwab.

Altogether Carnegie forced out some fifteen partners. Only the last of Carnegie's chairmen, Schwab, survived the office. All the others died or resigned under pressure. Carnegie made his presence felt also in the lower ranks. In 1895, for example, he ordered the board to fire the manager at Keystone Bridge, who had made a "sad showing." On the other hand, he continued his policy of making partners of "young geniuses," whom he discovered through cost sheets.

> Every year should be marked by the promotion of three or four of our young men. I am perfectly willing to give from my interest for this purpose when the undivided stock is disposed of. There is Miller at Duquesne, and Brown, both of whom might get a sixth of one percent.

And so on every year. The proportions sound minuscule, but in the 1890s even a sixth of 1 percent was worth hundreds of thousands of dollars; in addition there always existed the possibility of climbing higher after one got a foot on the bottom rung. Never forgetting his own excitement when he himself began to climb the "golden ladder,"

Carnegie at the top of that ladder carefully left it dangling where his subordinates could see it.

The surest way to move up, through a good showing on the cost sheets, Charlie Schwab understood thoroughly. He had come to Carnegie Steel as Bill Jones's protégé (he was Jones's grocery boy) and had risen from stake driver to assistant manager at Braddock in six months. In five years he became superintendent at Homestead. He combined Frick's greed, Jones's charm, and Carnegie's taste for empire with a better grasp of statistics, chemistry, and metallurgy than any of his superiors. Put in charge of Homestead after the strike, Schwab managed to get production up despite the hostility of the embittered work force. He cut costs $500,000 in 1895, primarily by substituting machines and unskilled workers for skilled labor, and by cutting the wages of all employees 15 percent, both of which he could accomplish unopposed with Amalgamated shattered by the strike. Carnegie, whose correspondence in the 1890s emphasized costs as fanatically as it had in the 1880s, described Schwab as "a wonder." As befitted a student of Captain Bill, Schwab also shared Carnegie's enthusiasm for modernized facilities. Between 1892 and 1900, Carnegie Steel replaced virtually its entire plant. At Duquesne, for example, the firm built blast furnaces equipped with automatic loading apparatus so efficient that the furnaces set world production records and cut labor costs 50 percent.

Carnegie pushed for improvements impatiently. In 1895 he wrote about a proposed rail mill, "Why should we wait till Fall to take up plans. . . . You should not lose a day. . . . Pray put this in train at once." He wanted more: "Now is the time to buy mills because we are in for a boom and big profits." When he took over the presidency, Schwab pushed even harder than Carnegie. In 1897 he announced to Carnegie that he wanted to build sixteen basic steel furnaces at Homestead to feed new angle and plate mills. He also wanted a new blooming mill at Homestead, and the Duquesne rolling mills remodeled to make nothing but sheets, angle bars, strips for pipe, and merchant steel, materials demanded in the new metropolitan markets of rapidly urbanizing America in which the urban population grew from 14 million in 1880 to 30 million in 1890.

As usual, Carnegie demanded to know not the costs of construction but the savings: "Your report should have given the figures upon which you base the opinion that the 'expenditure is desirable.' What we . . . ask is figures, not your opinion." Schwab supplied the figures; Carnegie conceded; the improvements went forward. Cost per ton at Homestead fell 34 percent in one year. The savings, reinvested in new blast furnaces, generated even better returns. Carnegie exulted—Schwab knew how to operate. "You are a hustler," he told him approvingly. "I am rejoicing at your brilliant success. . . . There has never been a time . . . that I can recall when everything seemed to be moving so smoothly."

While constantly revamping the plant and equipment, Carnegie Steel carried on an equally ambitious program with respect to raw materials. In 1892 the firm had ample supplies of the world's finest blast furnace coke through its control of Frick Coke Company. It paid $2.25 per ton for coke; British manufacturers paid $4.50 for a greatly inferior variety. Carnegie also had obtained easy access to plentiful limestone deposits by purchasing control of the Pittsburgh Limestone Company. The firm did not, however, have its own ore supply. Previous attempts to locate adequate deposits in Pennsylvania and West Virginia had failed. Like most of its competitors, Carnegie Steel had come to rely on ore from the Marquette region of Michigan.

By 1892 the firm consumed ore in quantities that were unimaginable a decade before. The firm's lack of an assured supply could render it exceedingly vulnerable when the Marquette deposits, once thought inexhaustible, disappeared into the insatiable maw of the American steel industry. Fortunately, explorations had located new deposits in Michigan (Gogebic, 1884), Wisconsin (Menominee, 1887), and Minnesota (Mesabi, 1891). Until 1892, however, technical and transportation problems precluded widespread use of these sources.

The Mesabi range proved to be the greatest bonanza ever struck for the American steel industry. The ore contained more than 60 percent iron; moreover, it lay on the ground, easily scooped up with a shovel, unlike most deposits, which required expensive, dangerous underground mining. The discoverers of the Mesabi deposits, the Merritt brothers of Duluth, faced great obstacles to successful exploitation of their find. The ore was so fine and powdery that skeptics said it could not be used in blast furnaces. The Merritts pressed on nonetheless, and acquired a large tract that they named Mountain Iron. It lay fifty miles from any form of transportation. They needed a railroad to the lake.

Lon Merritt went to Pittsburgh in 1891 hoping to convince Carnegie to supply the capital for opening up the region. Unfortunately, he saw not Carnegie, but Frick, who "did not use me like a gentleman, and cut me off short and bulldozed me." Rebuffed, Merritt returned north and built a railroad line with fast talk and faked credit. He got the first shipments out in 1892, and unleashed the rush. Furnace men adapted their equipment to Mesabi ore, for it cost 5 cents a ton to dig as opposed to $3 a ton for ore from underground mines. As pioneers, the Merritts occupied the most valuable sites in the regions, but in the fall of 1892 they desperately needed cash to keep digging.

Into the chaotic scene in Duluth walked Henry W. Oliver, world traveler, bon vivant, flamboyant winner and loser of a half-dozen fortunes—and flat broke again. Oliver wasted no time in cozying up to the Merritts—duck soup for the city slicker. Untroubled by his actual lack of funds, he gave the Merritts a worthless $5,000 check for a share in their partnership, and rushed back to Pittsburgh both to arrange a covering loan for the check and to persuade Carnegie Steel to reconsider. This time, Frick showed considerable interest. A year earlier, Lon Merritt had seemed a madman with a delirious tale of ore lying on the ground. Now Mesabi ore had become a reality; its cost offered enormous advantages to those who could get hold of it; when Oliver arrived the second time, Frick saw him as a godsend.

Carnegie, however, considered any deal with Oliver a shady proposition at best and an out-and-out swindle at worst. He and Oliver had been telegraph messenger-boys together. Fine. But Carnegie had subsequently gone "straight" while Oliver had turned into a speculator and a vagabond. Carnegie wanted no part of him: "Oliver's ore bargain is just like him—nothing in it."

Happily for the future of Carnegie Steel, Frick persisted, and Carnegie grudgingly yielded. Oliver made an irresistible offer—a half interest in the company he and the Merritts had formed in return for a $500,000 loan, secured by a mortgage on the ore properties. No sooner had the parties concluded this arrangement than came the depression of 1893. Facing bankruptcy, the Merritts and Oliver divided their property. John D. Rockefeller came to the Merritts' rescue and he got control of most of the Mesabi deposits, the railroad, and the ore loading docks. Carnegie Steel and Oliver held on to Oliver's share.

The emergence of Rockefeller as the controller of America's richest ore supply created an ominous spectacle for American steel manufacturers. Rockefeller quickly set up a line of ore boats on the lakes, and it looked to many as though he would duplicate his feats in the petroleum industry: first capture the sources of supply, second, the means of transportation. Then—who could tell? In 1894 Carnegie wrote, "Remember that Reckafellows [one of several Carnegie sobriquets for John D.] will own the R.R. and that's like owning the pipelines. Producers will not have much of a show."

In 1895 rumors circulated that Rockefeller intended to build a modern steel mill at Cleveland. Carnegie by now had become an advocate of backward integration. Shortly Oliver (representing Carnegie) and Frederick T. Gates (representing Rockefeller) opened negotiations. A confident Carnegie and his less sanguine partners wanted Rockefeller nailed down:

> HENRY CURRY: If we make this agreement it will [keep] Mr. Rockefeller out of the steel business.
>
> FRICK: If Rockefeller does not go into the steel business, someone else will.
>
> LEISHMAN: But very few people are hunting for places to invest an income of fifteen millions.

Finally Carnegie himself negotiated an agreement with "my fellow millionaire," as he sometimes addressed Rockefeller. Carnegie Steel leased the ore properties for fifty years, agreed to pay a royalty of 25 cents per ton of ore extracted, and promised to ship a minimum of 1,200,000 tons annually on Rockefeller's railroads and boat lines. Rockefeller in turn guaranteed that shipping charges would not exceed an agreed-on maximum. The last condition Carnegie thought particularly important. He would never have tied the company's future to a raw material supply without control of the shipping costs from the mines to the mills. He knew only too well how uncontrolled freight rates could undercut his competitive position, having battled the railroads for years on precisely that issue. Both parties had achieved their ends: Carnegie Steel got the ore at a fixed price without investing any capital (except for steam shovels), and Rockefeller secured a guaranteed annual revenue from his mineral deposits, boats, and railroads.

Iron Age, the industry's trade journal, called it Carnegie's greatest achievement: "It gives the Carnegie Company a position unequaled by any steel producer in the world." Carnegie enjoyed the position well enough, but he found equally satisfying his success with Rockefeller, whom he regarded as a tough, sharp operator. "Don't you know," he said, "it does my heart good to think I got ahead of John D. Rockefeller on a bargain."

The "bargain" had more profitable consequences than expected. News of the Carnegie–Rockefeller arrangement sent waves of panic through the ore region. Mine owners saw their best customer disappearing from the market with no replacement in sight. Oliver saw in their demoralization a further opportunity for moneymaking. He spent the summer arranging options on the best of the remaining independent mines, and the company managed to exercise the options, thereby completing its stranglehold on the richest ore deposits then known. The saving came to $1.50 per ton delivered at the mill over the price previously paid to independent mine operators.

The whole ore episode demonstrated an important dimension of the economic power of giant firms such as Carnegie Steel. Carnegie acquired exclusive rights to the Rockefeller ore without spending a cent, simply because he could promise to use 1,200,000 tons of ore every year for fifty years. No small firm could have signed such an agreement. Paradoxically, it would somehow have had to find the cash or credit to buy the property or a part of it outright. Size itself could thus contribute to economies of scale and facilitate growth. The compounded economies, when translated into reduced prices, made the efficiently managed giant firm a formidable competitor. The only hope for other firms in the industry lay in expanding themselves, usually by mergers, to achieve similar economies of scale. The result was oligopoly, competition among a small number of very large firms. Such industries dominated by a few very large firms have since become a familiar feature of the American business landscape—oil, rubber, automobiles, electrical equipment, to name but a few. Steel became the first concentrated American industry because of Carnegie's methods, which reshaped the field in less than thirty years. By the first decade of the twentieth century, the impact of these giants on American economy and society had emerged as the central issue in American life, dominating political campaigns from 1900 through 1914, fueling the rise of yet another reform party, the Progressives, provoking federal antitrust suits against such firms as Standard Oil and Du Pont, and precipitating a series of ever-tougher laws to control monopolies, regulate freight rates, and protect consumers against food and drug poisoning by greedy manufacturers.

In the van of the movement toward expansion and concentration, American steel producers quadrupled output while the number of producing units decreased by nearly one-fourth between 1870 and 1900. The growth in output stemmed from the sixfold increase in average investment that resulted both from infusions of fresh capital and the consolidation of many single units into large firms. However noteworthy this swift growth of investment, output grew even faster, showing the effect of economies of scale. In 1870 the industry produced an average of 60 pounds of metal for each dollar invested; in 1900, 112 pounds per dollar. Carnegie's firm bettered these averages significantly: between 1880 and 1900, the average steel establishment tripled its investment; Carnegie's multiplied tenfold. In 1880 every dollar of Carnegie capital produced 70 pounds of steel; in 1900, 153 pounds. Carnegie Steel set a torrid pace that forced the creation of other large firms.

In the same twenty-year period Carnegie's cost per ton of rail produced fell from $28.00 to $11.50, largely as a result of refurbishing equipment, expanding facilities, and integrating supplies. Some of the savings, however, resulted from improvements in transportation. By the spring of 1896 the firm's cost for both coke and iron ore had fallen to $2.50 a ton delivered in Pittsburgh. Although these prices afforded Carnegie Steel a favorable position vis-à-vis its rivals, Carnegie knew they included 55 cents shipping charges for each ton of coke and $1.15 for each ton of ore, and he sought to slash the freight charges. Carnegie carried on a relentless battle with the railroads. Because he knew so much about the way they operated, he often lost the sense of shrewd opportunism with which he dueled other antagonists. His attacks on the railroads frequently took the form of emotional, almost hysterical tirades that often embarrassed his associates.

His particular *bête noire* was his former employer, the Pennsylvania. Although he had hoped that the Braddock location on two railroads would give him the benefits of a competitive situation, it rarely worked out that way. The Baltimore and Ohio offered poor service and often could not supply the cars needed. As the steel firm expanded, its dependency on the Pennsylvania increased, exacerbating the conflict. Both Carnegie Steel and Frick Coke extracted rebates from the railroads whenever possible; railroads also took their pound of flesh where they could.

Carnegie insisted that the railroads cheated him. In 1884 he complained about rate discrepancies to Frank

Thomson, Pennsylvania Railroad vice-president, and warned that every manufacturer "in Pittsburgh . . . will rise in indignation. It is infamous and I gave you due notice you can't impose upon us." The Pittsburgh manufacturing community rising in its wrath to smite the "infamous" Pennsylvania was the specter that Carnegie repeatedly conjured up to bring the railroad to heel. That discriminatory rates existed no one could deny. It cost less, for example, to ship barrels of flour from Pittsburgh to Philadelphia by barging them first to Cincinnati than it did to send them direct by rail. Also, the railroad knew it could get away with charging $1 for 55 miles westbound and 90 cents for 75 miles eastbound on the same commodity because it had a monopoly. Carnegie shipped his goods that way or not at all.

In 1884 Carnegie in frustration departed from his usual policy of investing only in the steel company's properties. In that year the Pennsylvania and the New York Central, which had hitherto followed a policy of peaceful coexistence, invaded each other's territory. The Pennsylvania backed a new railroad, the New York, West Shore, and Buffalo. In retaliation, William Vanderbilt of the Central bought the long-dormant charter of the South Pennsylvania Railroad, which stipulated the right to build a line from Harrisburg to Pittsburgh.

Vanderbilt asked Carnegie for support. Carnegie, with visions of sinking freight rates dancing before his eyes, rounded up a group of Pittsburgh businessmen who contributed $5 million. Construction began immediately in the summer of 1884. Carnegie urged haste. Hoping to forestall this new competitor, the Pennsylvania dropped its rates as the construction crews toiled on. Delighted by this turn of events, in December 1884 Carnegie wrote George Roberts, the Pennsylvania's president, "There remains . . . only one survival of the previous [rate] policy which made every manufacturer in Pittsburgh a bitter enemy of the Penna R.R. Co."

Smugness soon gave way to consternation after a few months when all construction halted—Carnegie's pet scheme had received a mortal blow from a former ally, J. P. Morgan. As the man chiefly responsible for maintaining the reputation of major American railroad securities among European investors, Morgan thought the two rivals' invasion of each other's territories idiotic, and determined to put a stop to it. At a conference aboard his yacht the *Corsair* he browbeat the parties into a truce. The two railroads exchanged the rival properties; each was then free to do as it wished. The New York Central finished the West Shore as far as Albany. The Pennsylvania abandoned the South Pennsylvania's roadbed and tunnels to the groundhogs and bats. (In the twentieth century it became the route of the Pennsylvania Turnpike.)

The Pennsylvania promptly put its rates back up, and Carnegie returned to the attack. Since nothing else availed, he, like so many of his less wealthy fellow citizens, turned to the state, allying himself with disenchanted farmers, merchants, and manufacturers whose odyssey through the uncharted regions of railroad rate making had paralleled his own and had led them to agitate for state and federal regulation. The apogee of his campaign came in 1889 when he addressed the Pennsylvania State Legislature. Describing the Pennsylvania's behavior as "monstrous," he claimed that since the railroad lost money everywhere except in Pennsylvania itself, the road in effect levied a tax on the state's businesses in order to subsidize their competitors. He demanded legislation and threatened mob violence if it did not pass: "The people of Pittsburgh lined the streets on a memorable occasion before the [Confederate] rebellion broke out. . . . Are they to be forced into a similar protest against the Pennsylvania Railroad?"

This outburst distressed Frick, who viewed the railroad as a customer as well as a means of reaching markets. He favored negotiation and cooperation: "Our interests lie in the future with the P.R.R." Frick held too tenaciously to the doctrine of property rights to view Carnegie's blustering about mob violence with anything but distaste. He, Phipps, and Lauder tried to persuade Carnegie that an angry mob made a very blunt instrument of reform—one could never be certain that the firebrands would not next get shoved under one's own doors. Only Carnegie felt sure enough of the public's esteem to gamble that a mob would leave his property undisturbed. Carnegie had also demanded that the railroad's profits be controlled by statutes, another anathema to Frick. But Carnegie's crusade failed—the railroad had much more legislative influence in Pennsylvania than Carnegie Steel.

Frick had a more practical strategy for reducing transportation expenses. Soon after becoming chairman, he found that a very large share of costs arose from intramill and interplant switching. Trains hauled ingots from blast furnaces to rolling mill within each steel plant, for example, and carried beams from Homestead to Keystone Bridge. For these and hundreds of other indispensable moves the railroad naturally levied a high charge.

To cut the cost of moving the company's material around its own installations, Frick built the Union Railway, which connected all Carnegie Steel's scattered establishments to the area's trunk line railroads and performed all switching in the plants. So extensive were these movements that Union Railway operated one hundred miles of track and handled sixteen million tons of traffic in 1899—as much as the Northern Pacific, Union Pacific, and Missouri Pacific combined. The saving on freight charges alone paid for the investment. Added benefits flowed from the unification of traffic control under a single agency.

Completion of the Union Railway still left Carnegie dependent on the Pennsylvania to haul the coke up from Connellsville and the ore down from Lake Erie. Carnegie badly wanted to know how much the Pennsylvania's charges for these hauls handicapped him, so he ordered his own freight agent, George McCague, to ferret out his competitors' rates. McCague soon brought the word. (Carnegie must have been pleased with McCague, for his name appears on the 1899 list of partners with a share worth $451,000.) The word was bad. Carnegie Steel's transportation cost for the raw materials required to make a ton of steel exceeded Youngstown Steel's by 36 cents per ton, and Lorain Steel's by $1.10.

His worst suspicions thus confirmed, Carnegie had no mind to accept the conciliatory comments that Frick and McCague attached to the memo. "The P.R.R. . . . [has] pursued a liberal policy toward us during recent years," said McCague. Added Frick: "The Pennsylvania has been really assisting us . . . and they will do everything possible to assist this concern in holding its own against all comers. . . . It has been our policy to tie to them." Since railroads habitually followed a policy of generosity if not downright bribery toward the freight agents of major customers, and the Pennsylvania gave Frick Coke large rebates, both men may have spoken out of self-interest. Carnegie, who doubtless suspected as much, remained obdurate, and when the arrangement with Henry Oliver pointed toward even heavier ore traffic from the lake ports to Pittsburgh, Carnegie renewed his efforts to break the Pennsylvania's monopoly. He would not commit himself to buying Rockefeller's ore until he had, at long last, resolved the dilemma. In April 1894 Carnegie wrote disparagingly about the potential value of the ore discoveries: "This ore venture, like all our other ventures in ore, will result in more trouble and less profit than almost any other branch of our business." But by October 1896 he was ready, and he wrote Rockefeller, "I believe that you and I could fix it [the ore agreement] in a few minutes." This change in attitude stemmed from the fact that he had finally found a leash strong enough to bring his archenemy, the Pennsylvania, to heel.

The long-sought instrument of liberation from the Pennsylvania's clutches was a another railroad, the Pittsburgh, Bessemer, and Lake Erie, which Carnegie forged out of a strip of rusty iron pretentiously called the Pittsburgh, Shenango, and Lake Erie Railroad. The Shenango ran from Butler, Pennsylvania, thirty miles north of Pittsburgh, to Conneaut, Ohio, on Lake Erie. Its railroad line had deteriorated; its harbor facilities at Conneaut remained undeveloped; and it teetered on the edge of bankruptcy. All these problems notwithstanding, Carnegie wanted it badly, because it offered a two-edged sword with which to hack at the Pennsylvania. By building an extension from Butler to Bessemer where it would connect with the Union, Carnegie would have his own line from lake port to blast furnace, thus reducing shipping costs for ore. But he would also have a lever with which to budge the Pennsylvania on all its rates, because the Shenango crossed four other east–west lines—the Erie, the Wabash, the Nickel Plate, and the Lake Shore Railroads. Once he had a choice of several connecting lines over which to dispatch his freight, Carnegie felt confident the Pennsylvania would become more tractable.

To get control of the Shenango, Carnegie borrowed $1 million from United States Trust Company in New York, using Frick Coke Company stock as collateral. This million and two more from his personal funds quickly resuscitated the old line and built the new extension to

Bessemer. Now ready, Carnegie wrote Frick, "I do not blame Mr. Roberts [the Pennsylvania's president] for getting the best rates [he] can from us. . . . I quite appreciate this. I [myself] would not reduce rates until I thought it was necessary."

He wrote Frank Thomson, the Pennsylvania's vice-president, in more severe tones on May 5, enclosing a copy of the contract for the extension of the Shenango into Pittsburgh: "The Pennsylvania Road cannot afford to stand by and see its principal customers assailed by competitors who get lower rates." He would no longer have to put up with it because he would "get equal rates as soon as our line is finished to a connection with the Baltimore and Ohio, New York and Erie, Nickel Plate and the Lake Shore. Two of these have already told how anxiously they wait our coming." And the other roads wanted to haul not only his ore and finished products:

> You will observe that coke is also part of the contract. An extension to the coke region was part of the scheme [and] it will . . . be promptly done unless the matter is closed between us by Saturday. . . . I have only to say the word when I go to Pittsburgh on Monday.

Finally, just one more rattle of the Radical sword:

> The idea that Chicago can send ten thousand tons of plates to Newport News for three dollars a gross ton and the P.R.R. Co. tried to get four dollars net ton [from us]; and that billets reach New Jersey as cheaply from Chicago as from Pittsburgh! If the thousands of idle men in Pittsburgh today knew that this was one reason for its idleness, I would not give much for the receipts of the Pennsylvania Road in and around Pittsburgh. . . . Something must be done soon or an explosion will take place.

Thomson and Roberts had never shown much fear of explosions in Pittsburgh, but the threat of competition got their attention, for in Carnegie Steel they had the largest single freight customer in the world. They invited Carnegie to call at the railroad's headquarters in Philadelphia. Previously Carnegie had tried to see Roberts to air complaints but had met curt refusal; "I have enough business of my own to attend to Andy, I don't wish to have anything to do with yours." This time his hosts sang a different tune. As Carnegie recalled it (doubtless nothing was lost in the retelling), he got a cordial reception in Roberts's office. After the formalities, Thomson asked him: "What are you fighting the Pennsylvania Railroad for? You were brought up in its service. We were boys together. [This Thomson was J. Edgar's nephew.] Carnegie pulled out the list of his competitors' rates, handed them to Thomson, and said, "Well, Frank, I knew you would ask me that and here is the answer."

Confronted by their biggest customer, who now had alternative routes and information on rates to strengthen his hand, Roberts and Thomson quickly negotiated an agreement acceptable to Carnegie. They cut the ore rate from $1.15 to $0.63 a ton, coke from $0.55 to $0.35, and limestone from $0.80 to $0.55. Carnegie in return agreed not to build any more railroads or allow any of the Pennsylvania's competitors to build lines into his plants. The new agreement saved $1.5 million annually on raw material costs and even more after 1898, when the ore rate fell to $0.53. The Pennsylvania also agreed to give Carnegie Steel's finished products rates per ton mile equal "to those given . . . in other districts to steel manufacturers upon similar traffic." This understanding was meant "to bring the PRR and the CS Co. into close alliance," and was "never to be referred to." With this "close alliance" established, Carnegie wrote Thomson in tones very different from the calumny of the past decades, referring to "the dear old Pennsylvania Rail Road," which he hoped would "get a great deal more traffic than ever," and offering

Thomson "sincere congratulations upon the obvious success of your administration."

Under the Carnegie auspices, the Shenango soon emerged totally revitalized with new roadbed, cars, locomotives, and technical facilities. It became the most efficient in the world in terms of costs per ton mile and freight-train loads. Carnegie had not forgotten how to run a railroad. He moved James H. Reed from the Union Railway over to the Pittsburgh, Bessemer, and Lake Erie and then prodded him incessantly for results. Reed remarked that he expected it; "I know the 'Carnegie rule' is no credit for what has been done, but constant spurring for the future."

In the spring of 1898 the firm bought the whole Conneaut Harbor area and spent $250,000 to expand and modernize the ore-handling equipment. Rebuilt, it could empty a sixteen-thousand-ton ship of ore in fourteen hours, loading twenty freight cars an hour at the same time. In 1898 Carnegie forged the last link in the transportation chain by buying a fleet of ore boats to carry all tonnage above the commitment to the Rockefeller lines. Altogether the firm spent approximately $6.5 million on its transportation facilities exclusive of the Union Railway. The new equipment saved more than $2 million per year on the cost of raw materials, a better than 30 percent return on investment, presenting another excellent example of the advantages of the economies of scale available to those who can afford the equipment needed to achieve them.

In order to maximize the benefits of modernization and integration, the firm had to adapt its sales methods to meet changing markets. In the 1880s American railroads laid 76,000 miles of new track; in the 1890s, only 26,000. The depression of 1893, moreover, bankrupted dozens of railroads, which, along with generally depressed revenues,

reduced the demand for rails to replace worn-out track.
Consequently, in the 1890s, rails accounted for a declining
share of the firm's sales. In 1899, 50 percent of its output
consisted of other products, primarily materials required
for the expanding cities, including beams for skyscrapers;
girders for elevated railways; pipes for gas, water, and
sewage. Schwab had converted Homestead in 1897 to supply these items. The changing product line did not require
a new basic sales strategy; that remained constant—cut the
prices and move the goods—but it did demand a new
administrative structure.

When rails accounted for most of the sales, the firm had
relied primarily on the efforts and influence of Carnegie
and on its low prices to bring in the business. With most
rails sold in large lots and the contracts negotiated at high
executive levels, Carnegie often dealt with the railroad
presidents themselves. The firm sold most of its other
products through city commission merchants, who sold
the products of many different firms. They received no
salary, only a small commission (usually 1 percent).

The arrangement worked satisfactorily as long as most
of Carnegie Steel's nonrailroad output consisted of semi-
finished products such as billets sold to firms like Lukens
Steel, which manufactured boiler plate. The products were
simple and the transaction straightforward, the price being
the principal sales inducement. The firm paid its agent a
commission for taking the order, sending it on to Pittsburgh, and checking on delivery.

In the 1890s these arrangements began to change. As
sales in cities grew, the cost in agents' commissions rose
beyond the cost of establishing a company-operated sales
office. Furthermore, more complex products required that
people with technical background be available to consult
with customers; by the late 1890s Carnegie's sale offices
always included one expert on structural steel. Finally,
increased competition made it essential to have a qualified

representative exclusively devoted to selling Carnegie products.

The firm usually established a branch sales office by asking the firm's local commission merchant to change roles. Since Carnegie Steel seemed more agreeable as an employer than as a competitor, most merchants joined when asked. The possibility of becoming a partner dangled an added inducement. A. R. Whitney of New York, J. O. Hoffman of Philadelphia, and J. C. Fleming of Chicago began as commission merchants in the 1880s, became company sales agents in the early 1890s, and had partnership shares worth more than a million dollars each in 1899. By the end of the nineteenth century Carnegie Steel had its own offices in all the major cities in the United States and Canada and a general sales agent in Pittsburgh who sent out weekly bulletins outlining market prospects and haranguing the troops in the classic Carnegie style. The sales agent attended meetings of the board, as did salesmen partners when the occasion warranted.

The same pattern of sales development characterized the firm's entry into foreign markets. Carnegie deprecated the value of foreign trade until the 1890s. In 1889 he said, "We hear so much of foreign commerce . . . and yet [this] noisy branch counts for less than 5 percent [of all trade]." "Bad days for us when we have to take foreign trade," he said on another occasion. In the 1890s he became much less persnickety and would take business anywhere. The firm sold rails in Japan and China, for example. As business trickled in from far afield, Carnegie did one of his about-turns, waxing enthusiastic—"Send not less than five thousand tons into the British market no matter what we lose" and "Sell a limited amount of product to foreign markets even though prices are low just so as to keep up connections there."

The "connections" were commission merchants, granted exclusive franchises to sell Carnegie products in foreign countries. The board of managers cautioned the general sales agent to stand by this policy, thereby avoiding "any expense to establish agencies." Schwab, who believed in foreign trade and told Frick at one point, "We are going to control the steel business of the world," also favored using merchants. He pointed out that they had broken into the Latin American market that way, with a "very satisfactory arrangement with a firm of Commission Agents in Mexico City. We are at no expense." By the end of the century Carnegie Steel had such arrangements with steel merchants on every continent to complement its sales offices in North America.

By the late 1890s, as the United States contemplated entry into the arena of world powers, Carnegie Steel had created the most impressive industrial unit in the world, unsurpassed in what Carnegie designated "stage one," securing raw materials, and "stage two," the processing of raw materials into steel, as well as in the transportation networks that tied the two operations together. On the banks of the Youghiogheny and the shores of the Great Lakes, the firm controlled the largest and richest beds of coking and iron ore then known. In the Pittsburgh area it had the most modern steel-manufacturing facilities, fabricating bridges, turning out rails, structural shapes, billets, bars, sheets, and strips, and outproducing the total steel industry of Great Britain by 700,000 tons annually. The firm's switching railroad in Pittsburgh connected all its plants; its line from Pittsburgh to Lake Erie ran more cheaply than any railroad in the world. Its fleet of lake boats kept that part of transportation costs to a minimum. The compounded savings were such that in 1894, a depression year, Carnegie Steel had a net profit of $4 million, while its largest competitor, Illinois Steel, showed a $1 million loss. The following year Carnegie made $5 million; Illinois, only $360,000. The results of efficiency and reinvestment, the economies of scale brought in a flood of profits: 1895, $5 million; 1896, $6.7 million; 1897, $7 million; 1898, $11.5 million; 1899, $21 million; 1900, $40 million.

Forty million dollars. A contemporary observer declared, "Such a magnificent aggregation of industrial power has never before been under the domination of a single man"; and Carnegie echoed, "Where is there such a business!" The achievement was all the more impressive because during the years of greatest success, 1897–1900, the firm beat off the concerted attacks of its greatest competitors to date, leaving them in confusion and disarray.

The Peace Palace at The Hague, built with Carnegie funds (photographed in 1923)

X I

The Climb Ends

In 1898, while the United States broke its long detachment from conflict outside its continent by fighting the Spanish-American War, Carnegie, with new competitors looming on the horizon, announced "stage three" of the steel industry. "The next step—and it is coming, is to go into the manufacture of finished articles. . . . The concern that does this first will finish first." To Schwab he sent detailed instructions. He wanted to sell finished railroad cars "as soon as you can do it," as well as wire, nails, and boilers. He hoped members of the board would suggest other special articles, because "the concern that sells articles finished will be able to run all weathers and make some money while others are half-idle and losing money."

The man was 63 years old and spoiling for a fight. For years he had wanted to retire, but first labor troubles, then the depression had thwarted him. Determined to go out on top, on his own terms, he had to postpone his departure once more while he dealt with his competitors and his partners. In making these fresh challenges, Carnegie had no plan to act defensively; only to attack. Schwab, as usual, needed no urging. But there was dissension in the ranks, for Frick, Phipps, and Lauder all wanted to quit. Frick wanted to cash in, go to New York, collect paintings, and be a capitalist. Phipps and Lauder wanted to enjoy their long-awaited prosperity. They all knew that the new call to arms would mean confiscating all profits to buy more weaponry for the impending battle.

The lack of dividends had long chafed Phipps and Lauder. In 1884 Phipps had written Carnegie:

> Troubles unnumbered—unending, life too short, the game not worth the candle. When fair times come again, an arrangement can be made whereby we can have a haven of enjoyment and rest, instead of what may beset us any day, a sea of trouble, cares, and anxieties. To some plan of sale and security you, Dod and I should certainly look within the next year or two.

In 1895 Phipps wrote Carnegie again, laboring at the same metaphor:

> Quite sympathize with Jack's [John Vandevort's] wish for money—he is tired—discouraged with expansion. Hope tells a flattering tale, never otherwise with us. We get in sight of divd. then like Philip Nolan ("man without a country") he sees his native land—then a new ship, a new voyage—and never lands, each time a new and deeper disappointment, so with our divd.

Lauder wrote in the same vein.

> I have a long communication from Harry on the question of dividends v. improvements. His position seems to me unassailable. . . . I cannot see why you do not make dividends. . . . There is between 6 & 7 millions [surplus available]. . . . Why do you not make dividends?

He did not make dividends because he made improvements, and the bigger the profits, the bigger the improvements. The bigger the improvements, the more terrified the timid Phipps became. When he heard Schwab's 1897 expansion program, Phipps expostulated, "My breath was taken away. Better some opportunities be missed, than this fast jumping at things. . . . By all means do let us go a little slower, my heart is often in my mouth when I read of their rushing way in big things." Phipps had long since become too weary to crave the call to battle. Now his general wanted to mount a new campaign. Once again the shore, the haven of peace, quiet retirement, and, above all, wealth were receding into the distance.

Could Phipps have sold his interest at a fair market value, he would have. Unhappily for him, he could not, because the "Iron Clad Agreement" bound him and all the other partners. This document, originally drawn up in 1887, had three main provisions. First, if a partner died, the remaining partners had the right to buy his shares at "book" value, and they had an extended time period to pay for them. If Carnegie died, for example, his stock became the firm's property, and the company had fifteen years to pay his heirs for it. For the other partners the duration of payment was prorated according to the size of their holdings. The agreement's second provision stated that at any time a partner could be forced to sell his interest back to the company at book value by a two-thirds vote of his partners. Since Carnegie owned 58 percent, he could not be expelled; no other partner could be ejected without his consent; and in theory at least he alone could not force anyone out. In practice, of course, if Carnegie wanted a man out, he went. Third, the agreement provided that a partner who wanted to retire could sell out, but he had to accept book value and collect it in installments.

The Iron Clad protected the other partners in the event of Carnegie's death. Without the provision for time payments, the surviving partners would probably have had to sell the business to pay Carnegie's share to his heirs. This danger had brought the agreement into being in the first place, because Andrew Carnegie had nearly died of typhoid in 1886 at the same time that Tom had his final illness. Phipps, badly frightened by the complications he foresaw if both brothers died simultaneously, had therefore pressed for the Iron Clad. The agreement also made it impossible for outsiders to acquire any share of the firm. Only partners could hold an interest, and they controlled access to the firm. Carnegie, as controlling partner, had no intention of relinquishing any interest in Carnegie Steel to "adventurers," "stockjobbers," or "speculators."

Phipps, the originator of the Iron Clad, now found himself snarled in its clauses. The provisions that most embarrassed him, Lauder, and Frick prohibited them from selling to outsiders and required them to take book value. Book value meant the partner's percentage of ownership times the nominal capitalization figure. In 1899, for example, Phipps held an 11 percent interest, and the firm's book capital was $50 million. If he had sold out, he would have received $5.5 million; Frick's 6 percent equaled $3 million; Lauder's 4 percent $2 million; and so on.

The undeniable fact that the company's real worth greatly exceeded the book figure whether calculated on the basis of asset value, earning potential, or market value infuriated this trio. In 1899 Phipps and Frick thought Carnegie Steel worth $250 million, quite a reasonable estimate based on its $21 million profit for the year. At that figure Phipps held an interest worth $27.5 million, Frick $15 million, and Lauder $10 million. Carnegie, however, held down the firm's book value. He saw no reason to enlarge it; overcapitalization smacked of speculation. The country teemed with jury-rigged amalgamations "manufacturing nothing but stock," as Carnegie put it. Although he toyed with recapitalization schemes, his partners despaired of ever generating a solution internally.

The only possible salvation, it seemed to Phipps's group, lay in finding an outside buyer who would offer Carnegie a deal he could accept. The "Old Man" had often spoken of retirement. He had no son to succeed him, and in the

To Carnegie's grim satisfaction, the team of Frick, Phipps, Gates, and the Moores could not raise $57 million cash. No banker, Morgan included, would touch the proposition because of its dubious promoters. The spectacle of the unhappy consortium vainly hawking his company through New York's financial highways and byways chagrined Carnegie no small amount, but not nearly so much as if they had succeeded in raising the money.

When it became clear that the anticipated banking support would not materialize, the anxious syndicate decided to try it on their own by chartering a Pennsylvania corporation authorized to issue $250 million in stock and $100 million in bonds. They hoped that Carnegie would take the bonds and that the investing public would swallow enough stock to generate the $57 million cash to which he was also entitled.

Carnegie found some distressing revelations in the details of the new proposal. Of the proceeds, he discovered $15 million earmarked for expenses. That alone confirmed Carnegie's distaste for such transactions; the amount allotted for "expenses" to set up the new firm equaled one-third of its physical assets. Worse yet, the lawyer would get $250,000 of these "expenses"; the balance divided into thirds, "One third . . . for Moore," wired Frick and Phipps, "one third for us," and then—as an obvious ploy to distract Carnegie from that bit of knavery—"one third to be held for deserving young men, thus carrying out your long cherished idea."

This skulduggery did not escape Carnegie. He wrote on the back of the cable, "Frick and Phipps. Secret bargain with Moore's to get large sum for obtaining option. Never revealed to their partners." In Carnegie's view the two had become "promoters" with a strong vested interest in consummating a shabby bargain that would have turned the company over to professional speculators. Carnegie waited impatiently for Wall Street's verdict. It was negative;

indigestion yet prevailed. Frick and Phipps came to Skibo to request an extension of the option. Carnegie replied succinctly, "Not an hour!"

In due course the option expired, and $1,170,000 went into the Carnegie account, to the great annoyance of Frick and Phipps; the $1,170,000 had come out of their own pockets. Carnegie had agreed verbally to refund any portion of the option money put up by his partners, but he reneged when he learned of their perfidy in writing themselves a $5 million bonus into the deal. Phipps especially suffered from the confiscation; he had raised his share with difficulty, and the loss of it pained his miserly soul. Carnegie derived a savage satisfaction from administering the comeuppance. In later years he liked to give his guests a tour of Skibo and then, when they admired the estate, describe it as "a little present from Mr. Frick."

Poorer if not wiser, Frick and Phipps scurried about in search of new and more viable arrangements. Probably Carnegie decided to dispose of Frick once and for all as soon as the details of the abortive transaction became clear. He had had the chance in 1894 and passed it up, granting Frick the face-saving sop of board chairmanship and leaving him in charge of the Coke Company. In the latter role he had functioned well, but Carnegie entertained no illusions about Frick's indispensability. He could replace Frick at any time with one of his ambitious young "associates."

As long as his successor, the timid Leishman, held the presidency, Frick played a more active role as chairman of the board than Carnegie had contemplated. Schwab, however, changed matters when he replaced Leishman. Tough, aggressive, ambitious, and equipped with more finesse than Frick, he took the reins firmly in hand. Frick proposed, but Schwab disposed, and Carnegie backed him up. When the final collision came, Schwab lined up firmly at Carnegie's side.

Once Carnegie had learned of Frick's dishonesty, he allowed him no further voice in the firm's management. Carnegie had shown in the past that he would brook no such behavior on the part of his associates. Whenever he felt that a subordinate's conduct reflected unfavorably on himself or his business, Carnegie invariably reacted ruthlessly. In his mind his own self-interest came before justice, loyalty, gratitude, or friendship. The Iron Clad, for example, had bitten the unhappy Leishman for his speculative roguery. Carnegie bided his time looking for a suitable issue to precipitate the ultimate quarrel with Frick.

A man in such a temper rarely has to wait long, and a chance soon arrived. In the final dispute between the two, Carnegie behaved much as Frick had during the Homestead strike: he took a position so outlandish that it forced his opponent to extreme measures, thereby justifying forceful retaliation. Coke, appropriately enough, furnished the substance of the terminal collision. Carnegie and Frick had made a verbal agreement that beginning January 1, 1899, Carnegie Steel would pay $1.35 per ton to Frick Coke for the next three years. Both men soon regretted the bargain: Carnegie, because Phipps pointed out that if the market price fell the steel company would suffer; Frick, because in fact the price went up, not down. Soon the coke company began billing the steel company at higher prices than the "contract" called for: $1.45, $1.60, then $1.75. Even the last figure fell well below the prevailing market price; nevertheless, it violated the understanding. The steel company's treasurer, well aware of his overlord's gimlet-eyed perusal of the cost sheets, refused to pay the bills.

As chairman of the coke company, Frick forthwith declared that he would ship no more coke to the steel company, which he also served as chairman. Chief victim of this impasse was Schwab, the operating head of the steel firm. In order to keep rolling (this after all was a $21 million profit year), Schwab cut the Gordian knot by telling the treasurer to pay the bills, but to mark all amounts over $1.35 per ton "payments on advances only." Lauder, whose chief role was that of executive-level spy on his colleagues, kept Carnegie informed of this jockeying. "No sir," wrote Carnegie, "Frick can't repudiate contracts for any company which myself and friends control. We are not that kind of cats."

Like angry Pharisees both combatants now invoked the letter of the oft-violated law. Carnegie said Frick must uphold the contract. Frick said that neither he nor Carnegie had authority to make contracts, and since both firms' bylaws designated the officer with such authority, nothing they had agreed to could be enforced. The patent absurdity of both positions testified to the commitment both men had to the collision course on which they had set themselves. Further tribulations soon arose. The Carnegie Company wanted to buy a mill site at Peters Creek; Frick, it developed, already owned it. The company bought it and Frick pocketed a nice profit. In conversation with friends Carnegie denounced Frick's real estate purchase as an "improper act." That did it.

Frick arrived at the next Carnegie board meeting, boiling with wrath, and flayed Carnegie:

> I learn that Mr. Carnegie while here said I showed cowardice in not bringing up the question of the price of coke. . . . He also stated that he had his doubts as to whether I had any right, while Chairman of the Board of Managers of the Carnegie Steel Company to make such a purchase [as the land at Peters Creek]. Why was he not manly enough to say to my face what he said behind my back? . . . Harmony is so essential for the success of any organization that I have stood a great many insults from Mr. Carnegie in the past, but I will submit to no further insults in the future.

Thus unburdened, he stalked out of the board room, never to return.

The final battle lines drawn, the minions hastened to encourage their leader. Lauder wrote Carnegie:

> No one in our firm has given as much trouble as Mr. Frick has done. . . . This present angry craziness . . . seems to be prompted altogether by personal feeling. . . .
>
> Would any possible sacrifice . . . be too much . . . to cut loose altogether from such a disturbing element? . . . The Chairman seems to have burned his boats. . . . The issue is now Carnegie or Frick pure and simple.

Carnegie had often shown how he resolved such issues. He told Lauder, "You voice my views exactly. Frick goes out. . . . He's too old, too infirm in health *and mind.* . . . I have nothing but pity for Frick. . . . His recent exhibition is childish."

Carnegie knew, of course, that Lauder would support him. The support he had to have, however, was Schwab's, for he had decided to "tell C.M.S. [Schwab] he will be the man and the only man." The new "man" rallied round at once; Schwab knew the outcome of this struggle in advance and meant to be on the winning side. Wrote Schwab, "*I am always with you.* Aside from deep personal regard and feeling for you, you have heaped honors and riches upon me and I would indeed be an ingrate to do otherwise. . . . Believe me, my dear Mr. Carnegie, I am always with you and yours to command." He then outlined to Carnegie the other partners' predicament. They feared standing openly against Frick, lest an unexpected reconciliation leave them vulnerable to savage retribution.

> The boys are, I am sure, most loyal to you, but knowing Mr. Frick's power in the past will hesitate to do anything against him fearing the matter might ultimately be fixed up and . . . injure or end their careers. The only way for you to do is to take *decisive action yourself first.*

Schwab then wrote Frick, warning him that he intended to side with Carnegie in any showdown, "I can not possibly see any good to you or anyone else by doing otherwise. It would probably ruin me and not help you."

Assured of his chief lieutenant's backing, Carnegie moved swiftly. He demanded and got Frick's resignation from the Carnegie Steel Board of Managers. Next, he used his majority interest to pack the Frick Coke Company's board with his allies. Then, at the next meeting, this reconstituted tribunal rammed through a formal contract to sell Carnegie Steel all the coke it required at $1.35 per ton, and ordered a refund of all charges above that amount previously collected. At this point in the proceedings Frick jumped up, declared, "You will find there are two sides to this matter," and hurried to consult his lawyer about getting an injunction against the new coke contract.

The next morning, January 9, 1900, Carnegie appeared in Frick's office and played his trump card, the Iron Clad. Frick must drop his lawsuit, and accept the new agreement. "And if I don't," asked Frick, "what, then?" Then, Carnegie informed him, the company would take over his interest at book value. This of course was a devastating threat. Not only did the difference between book and market values amount to at least $10 million, but also expulsion at this point meant exclusion from a share of the company's profits in what bade fair to be its best year ever. This threat outraged Frick; he told Carnegie, "For years I have been convinced that there is not an honest bone in your body. Now I know that you are a god-damned thief. We will have a judge and jury of Allegheny County decide what you are to pay me."

Having received this volley, Carnegie withdrew to his redoubt and at once convened his docile board. They invoked the Iron Clad; Frick sued for a reevaluation of the firm's assets. It was the Shinn affair all over again, but for massively greater stakes.

Frick's brief shredded the shroud of secrecy that Carnegie Steel had carefully maintained over the years.

The firm's profits became common knowledge, with repercussions far and wide in American society. The newspapers seized gleefully on this bonanza, tailor-made for the heyday of the muckraker and yellow journalism. *Iron Age* lamented that what "has caused the most talk is the revealed profits of the Company. It has aroused all of the old anger against trusts." Fellow Pittsburgh industrialist George Westinghouse wrote offering to mediate; the Republican party quivered at this unseemly display of bitterness and greed by two of its stalwart supporters.

By mid-March tempers had cooled. On neutral ground in Atlantic City the disputants' representatives reached a compromise. They created a holding company, the Carnegie Company, which took control of Carnegie Steel and Frick Coke. The new company had a capitalization of $320 million, half common stock and half 5 percent bonds. Carnegie's share was $174,526,000; Frick's $31,284,000, considerably more than the $4.9 million he would have received under the Iron Clad. Schwab received a 2 percent interest ($6.4 million) as a reward for his loyalty and as an incentive for future prodigies of effort.

Carnegie had lost his treasured control of the size of the firm's capitalization. In fact, it now had the largest capitalization of any American manufacturing concern. But he had won much as well. He had purged Frick's disruptive presence permanently from the company's management; he had rewarded Schwab; he had achieved the recapitalization without paying a dime to bankers, promoters, or underwriters. The new arrangement automatically scrapped the Iron Clad Agreement; and although in theory Carnegie Company shares might have traded on the stock exchange, in fact they never did. Partly this resulted from Carnegie's cunning insistence that all the holding company's securities be issued in thousand-dollar denominations. That discouraged casual trafficking. Serious trading never got underway, because soon after the Frick issue's resolution

Carnegie completed the campaign that brought his manufacturing career to its triumphant conclusion. For the
duration of its existence the Carnegie Company's ownership remained in the hands of Andy and his "boys." And
Frick.

Six months after the signing of the protocol, Frick sent
a jibing cable to Carnegie: "Do not let them [Carnegie's
managers] hide things from you. You cannot trust many
by whom you are surrounded to give you the facts. . . .
You are being outgeneraled all along the line, and your
management of the company has already become the subject of jest." A hard man, Henry Frick, and he never laid
down his grudge. A tale eventually emerged that Carnegie,
late in life, sent Frick a note suggesting that since they both
had grown old they should bury the past and meet as
friends. Frick replied, "Tell Mr. Carnegie I'll meet him in
Hell."

This violent struggle between Carnegie and Frick was
an anachronistic island in the sea of industrial modernity
they had done so much to bring to flood tide. Their clash
was one of proprietary pride in an era of corporate ownership and bureaucratic anonymity. Frick Coke had long
since ceased to function as anything but an integrated cog
in the Carnegie Steel works, but Frick still felt as much
pride in it as he had on his thirtieth birthday when he
learned it had made him a millionaire.

Carnegie Steel had become the largest industrial unit in
the world. It employed 20,000 people, most of whom had
never seen Carnegie, but it bore his name and it had a mis-
sion in Carnegie's life. He, like Lauder, sought a haven of
rest, but only his business could carry him there. He had
so much to make up for: the failure of his father; the igno-
minious flight from poverty; the people ground up and fed
to his insatiable ambition—Woodruff, Kloman, Tom
Scott, his own brother Tom; the lies to get contracts; the
brutality to make them pay; the greed and the trickery;

and Homestead, always Homestead. But he could make up for it all with the wealth and the power that his company, his "concern" as he often called it, could bring him. It was the instrument of atonement, clean and hard and pure as American steel and the fire that made it. Frick, who had bloodied the instrument at Homestead, had tried to dip it into the filth of watered stocks and shoddy promotion. Carnegie had to reclaim it to protect his own redemption. The bitter battle even then belonged to the past as much as an encounter between dinosaurs. The new industrial titans already occupied the field, creating an obstacle Carnegie had to surmount to reach his destination.

In the late 1890s the steel processing and fabricating industries became dominated by newly created manufacturing trusts. Among them were the "Americans"—Steel and Wire, Steel Hoop, Steel Barrel, Sheet Steel, Tin Plate, which were the stepchildren of the Gates–Moore syndicate—and National Tube, American Bridge, and Federal Steel, assembled by J. P. Morgan. These concatenations resulted from years of competition in the 1870s and 1880s, followed by the stringencies of the depression of the nineties. It was this array of behemoths that lumbered out to do battle with Carnegie and Schwab.

The first encounter came in 1897 with Illinois Steel, a Chicago firm founded in 1889 and the Carnegie Company's largest competitor. Illinois Steel, like Carnegie Steel, produced mostly primary products: rails, billets, sheets, bars, and the like. Illinois, however, was on the verge of becoming a part of Federal Steel, a large complex that Morgan brought to fruition in 1898. Carnegie and Schwab saw clearly enough the direction in which these consolidations pointed—Illinois-Federal would become the first and second stages supplying the third-stage firms such as American Steel Hoop, thus closing off a large part of the Carnegie market. For this reason, Schwab, all through 1897, pushed to finish the expansion and conversion of Homestead. It also explains Carnegie's reaction when Illinois Steel suggested a pool to divide the heavy steel business. "Our policy in my opinion is to stand by ourselves alone. . . . Take orders East and West. . . . As for Illinois Steel: if you do arrange with them, you are simply bolstering a concern and enabling it to strike you in the near future." It would be foolish, Carnegie argued, to throw away the cost advantages they had worked so hard to build up over the years. "We have made the fight," he urged, "the enemy is at our mercy, now do not let us be foolish enough to throw away the fruits of victory."

In 1898 Federal Steel emerged from the Morgan shop; the other manufacturing trusts began to take shape; and Carnegie made his declarations about making wire, nails, and other finished articles. Carnegie knew the weakness of the new consortiums: vastly overcapitalized and inefficient; and they could not possibly compete with Carnegie Steel if it integrated forward into the manufacture of finished products. "It was," as the Stanley Committee characterized it, "a contest between fabricators of steel and fabricators of securities; between makers of billets and makers of bonds." In 1898 Carnegie said of Federal Steel, "I think Federal the greatest concern the world ever saw for manufacturing stock certificates. . . . But they will fail sadly in steel."

By the end of 1898 the trusts had begun beating at the gates: American Bridge Company wanted to absorb Keystone Bridge. Carnegie replied, "Surely my views about going into trusts are well known. . . . The Carnegie Steel Company should never in my opinion enter any Trust. It will do better attending to its own business in its own way. . . . We hope our competitors will combine, for an independent concern always has the 'Trust' at its mercy." Although new enemies sprang up daily, Carnegie concluded, "Prospects were never so bright."

Soon another antagonist appeared. American Tin Plate Company threatened to stop buying Carnegie's steel unless he agreed not to sell to other tin plate manufacturers. Here the enemy appeared in its most sinister form, exactly as Carnegie had predicted. Some of his partners favored the arrangement. He opposed it. "In these days of Trusts and other swindles I do not favor the contract as made; I do not believe it is legal; I do not believe it is right. I think the Carnegie Company should keep a pure record. . . . I believe that independent concerns will soon beat the trust."

He did his best to ensure just such an outcome. He joined plate, beam, and rail pools, then jumped out of them without warning, sending prices tumbling to levels where only he could operate profitably.

He gloried in the thrust and parry of mortal combat with the trusts. They were the enemy and he meant to whip them. He wrote John Morley in 1899, "I have had to take general charge of the business for next year. Some means to be made to meet these huge combinations which are really at our mercy. But my being at the helm makes victory easier. So thought my partners, but it is only a short postponement of withdrawal. Ashamed to tell you profits these days. Prodigious."

Carnegie's "prodigious" profits reached $21 million. He paid $5 million in dividends and poured the rest back into open hearth furnaces and other improvements, and none too soon. In 1900 the ultimate challenge came. National Tube, American Steel and Wire, and American Hoop canceled their steel contracts. They had built their own furnaces or had arranged to buy from Illinois Steel. Schwab urged the board of directors to hurry improvements. As always Lauder hesitated: "This is a very dangerous time in our history. . . . With . . . the very doubtful state that the business is in I think we should defer action." Schwab argued, "We have got to move . . . or shut down our plants. We have no outlet for our billets. . . . We have from 35,000 to 40,000 tons of steel that has been going into such products as wire, nails, hoops, etc. . . . Now we cannot sell the tonnage." He asked for $1.4 million to build rod, wire, and nail plants, and the board approved.

Carnegie urged them on with the old refrain: "run full; take orders; run full." In July when the contract cancellations began to come in, he wired, "Crisis has arrived, only one policy open; start at once hoop, rod, wire, nail mills. . . . Extend coal and coke roads, announce these; also tubes. . . . Have no fear as to result, victory certain. Spend freely for finishing mills, railroads, boat lines." Shortly he added:

> A struggle is inevitable, and it is a question of survival of the fittest. For many years we have seen that the manufacturer must sell finished articles . . . I would make no dividends upon common stock, save all surplus and spend it for a hoop and cotton tie mill, for wire and nail mills, for tube mills, for lines of boats upon the lakes.

At the root of his aggressive strategy stood, as usual, cold hard logic and a precise understanding of the situation. The combinations assembled by Gates, the Moores, and Morgan survived only in the absence of competition. A creaky collection of obsolete machinery (some of it dating back to the Civil War), they lay scattered randomly around the country, vastly overcapitalized. National Tube, for example, had a capital stock of $80 million to try to pay dividends on. Julian Kennedy, Morgan's expert on steel works (and a Carnegie-trained man), told Morgan that National Tube's nineteen plants had a market value of $19 million.

Carnegie knew that "the country cannot buy the total product of steel works"; therefore, financiers formed trusts to control prices by controlling output. Carnegie

Steel could "take the business at the best price possible and run the works full, independent of all other concerns, managing our own business in our own way," or it could "take percentages of the business with these [trusts] and try to maintain prices." Carnegie had no doubt about the proper course. In the past the decision to take orders and run had always triumphed. Carnegie Steel had unmatched facilities, adequate capital with profits pouring in, and an abundance of technological know-how. The trusts could not match it; they would go to the wall.

Schwab enthusiastically followed his leader, and together they began to fashion a weapon with which to mount a smashing attack, a new $12 million completely integrated tube plant on the firm's harborside property at Conneaut. Conneaut offered incomparable advantages for such a project: abundant iron ore, coke, and limestone shipped up at virtually no cost in the company's own empty ore cars returning for reloading. In addition, the lake shore site offered the advantage of cheap water transport for the finished products. Finally, the firm had acquired control of a new patented process for manufacturing seamless tubes, the closest approach to continuous flow manufacturing yet achieved in the steel industry. "How much cheaper, Charlie, can you make tubes than the National Company?" Carnegie asked Schwab, who answered, "At least $10 per ton." "Well," said Andy, "go and build the plant then." The firm's ability to achieve low costs and to estimate in advance had once again proved its worth.

Carnegie's plans to manufacture finished products sent the promoters rushing to Morgan for help. They knew they could not hope to compete. Under Carnegie's pressure their dilapidated contraptions would have imploded at once. Said one Morgan partner later, "When Andrew Carnegie gave his approval to the plant at Conneaut, he became an incorporated threat and menace to the steel trade of the United States." After Carnegie testified before his committee, Congressman Stanley said to him, "I believe you would have captured the steel trade of the world if you had stayed in business." Carnegie replied, "I am as certain of it as I can be certain of anything."

The most persuasive testimony to Carnegie's unassailable position came from Elbert Gary, who headed Federal Steel and subsequently became chairman of United States Steel. "It is not at all certain that if the management that was in force at the time had continued, the Carnegie Company would not have driven entirely out of business every steel company in the United States."

Soon the white flag rose over the enemy's battlements. On December 12, 1900, a group of New York bankers gave Schwab a testimonial dinner at the University Club. At Schwab's right sat J. P. Morgan. In his after-dinner remarks, Schwab expounded on the American steel industry of the future, on how both low prices and industry stability could be achieved through a complex, scientifically integrated firm supplanting the grotesque creations of stock certificate manufacturers. Morgan was intrigued. He invited Schwab to come to his home and elaborate on his plan in greater detail. Schwab came on an evening in January. The session lasted all night. Finally Morgan said, "Well, if Andy wants to sell, I'll buy. Go and find his price."

Schwab first talked to Mrs. Carnegie. He explained the situation and asked her for a prediction of Carnegie's reaction. Louise encouraged Schwab, offered her support, and suggested to Charlie that he approach Andy on the golf course, for "Doctor Golf" usually put Carnegie in a good humor. This Schwab did. Carnegie listened and asked Schwab to return the next day. When he came back, Carnegie handed him a piece of paper on which he had written in pencil,

Capitalization of Carnegie Company: $160,000,000 bonds to be exchanged at par for bonds in new company	$160,000,000
$160,000,000 stock to be exchanged at rate of $1,000 share of stock in Carnegie Company exchanged for $1,500 share of stock in new company	240,000,000
Profit of past year and estimated profit for coming year	80,000,000
Total price for Carnegie Company and all its holdings	$480,000,000

Carnegie attached only one other condition. His, Dod's, and Tom Carnegie's widow's shares were to be paid only in 5 percent, first-mortgage bonds. It was as simple as that. Andy knew how these things were done. Schwab carried the paper to Morgan, who glanced at it and said, "I accept this price." Thus United States Steel was born.

A few days later Morgan called on Carnegie to shake hands on the deal. "Mr. Carnegie, I want to congratulate you on being the richest man in the world." He had made it. Carnegie had fulfilled the American dream in its fullest glory—poor immigrant boy to richest man in the world. Carnegie sent the news to Phipps, sick with bronchitis. The long voyage had ended at last. Tom Miller's $800 loan had blossomed into $50 million: his $50 million. Phipps looked at the doctor who brought him the news, and choked, "Ain't Andy wonderful!" Carnegie himself seemed equally pleased with the outcome. "All seems well about the steel matter," he wired Dod Lauder, "no hitch—so be it."

The new company printed $300 million worth of bonds for Carnegie and put them in a vault in Hoboken. He never saw them, and he never touched them; he gave them away. In giving them away he found peace. He gave 3,000 libraries, costing $60 million, and used by millions of people a day. He gave 4,100 church organs. He founded Carnegie Trust for the Universities of Scotland, Carnegie Hall in New York, Carnegie Institutes in Pittsburgh and Washington. He established Carnegie School of Technology, and finally the Carnegie Foundation with an endowment of $125 million. He became a leader for world peace, and built the Peace Palace at The Hague in the Netherlands. He did all this and more before he died peacefully in his sleep on August 11, 1919. He did not die disgraced; he had given it all away. He thus created no Rockefeller-like dynasty. Louise lived until 1946; his daughter Margaret married happily and had four children of her own, none of them in the steel business.

It is right that he should be remembered for his philanthropies. He lived up to his own creed. But he should be remembered as a businessman as well. A child of the Old World, he did much to bring on the new one. He found the iron industry a collection of small, scattered enterprises; he left it a giant, integrated business. What he learned on the railroad he brought to manufacturing. In generations to come, others followed the trail of cost control, low prices, low profits, and high volume in building America into the world's richest society; Carnegie blazed it with vision, courage, and—undeniably—a cold detachment from the pain of those he trampled, rich or poor. Where he led, Henry Ford, Pierre du Pont, and the others followed.

A collection of paradoxes, this man of American steel— he showed himself violent and peace loving, ruthless and loyal, greedy and generous, boastful and diffident, vain and doubting, brash and shy. Like his adopted country and so many of its citizens past and present, he exhibited a curious mixture of Jeffersonian rhetoric and Hamiltonian action. In his life we may easily see reflections of ourselves and our past.

And now having talked about him for so long, I think I'll step back and give Andy the last word.

The eighth wonder of the world is this:

two pounds of iron-stone purchased on
the shores of lake Superior and
            transported to Pittsburgh;

two pounds of coal mined in Connellsville
and manufactured into coke and
            brought to Pittsburgh;

one half pound of limestone mined
east of the Alleghenies and
            brought to Pittsburgh;

a little manganese ore,
mined in Virginia and
            brought to Pittsburgh.

And these four and one half pounds of material
manufactured into one pound of solid steel
and sold for one cent.

That's all that need be said
            about the steel business.

Epilogue

Fifty years after Andrew Carnegie died, and shortly after the publication of the first edition of this book, foreign competition sent the traditional American steel industry into a near-death spiral. As steel poured in from Taiwan, Japan, Korea, and Poland, the American giants— Bethlehem, Republic, Jones and Laughlin, and even Carnegie Steel's successor, United States Steel—struggled for survival, shedding plants, workers, and managers through the 1970s and 1980s and calling for a restoration of tariff barriers to protect them. The American companies showed what critics—Henry Frick among them—had long suspected: big steel had followed not Carnegie's path but Morgan's, not competition, but co-existence. Shielded by politics and historical circumstance—tariffs, two world wars, a great depression—the American firms had lost both the taste and skill for competition.

Little survived from the Carnegie era but Carnegie's old plants, and in the heat of competition, they too gradually melted away until, when Boston public television station WGBH filmed a Carnegie documentary in 1995, little remained to film except rusting machinery and abandoned buildings. At Homestead, where Frick had destroyed the Amalgamated nearly a century before, the last mill closed in 1986, destroying the workers' community that had survived Frick, the Pinkertons, Schwab, and the Great Depression of the 1930s to prosper through the efforts of the United Steel Workers, a union that acquired a power the likes of which the Amalgamated's leaders had never dreamed.

The destruction of jobs in Homestead and other American steel towns illustrated the maxim that one should never ascribe to wickedness what can be explained by incompetence, for management ineptitude killed American steel jobs and the communities they supported. Watching this debacle, and having in a sense lived with Andrew Carnegie for so long, I imagined a conversation in which I said to him, "The Japanese haul in the raw materials from all around the world, process them in Nagasaki and Yokohama, ship them to the United States, undersell all the American firms, and make a profit doing it. What do you think of that, Andy?"

In my imagination Mr. Carnegie replied, "I think it's a great time to go into the steel business." And so it proved, for even as big steel failed, little steel succeeded, as "mini-mills" such as Chapparal Steel and Nucor, in the words of Chapparal's president, "went into the carbon-steel business when everyone else was getting out of it." As the big firms pleaded for protection, the president of Nucor described "intense competitive pressure" as the source of "a lot of things that are beneficial: more of an orientation toward technology, greater productivity . . . changes in management structure [because] the real impediment [is] management [that has] deeply ingrained habits [not] open to change. Above all, the new mills focused on costs, determined to produce steel for less than the transportation costs of Japanese steel."

In the success of the mini-mills, the Carnegie creed lives

on, doubtless to his great satisfaction wherever he may be, even if in Hell with Mr. Frick. In the resurgent American economy of the 1990s, the power of Carnegie's ideas has resurfaced in a multitude of industries, but for Carnegie himself, I'm sure nothing could equal the pleasure of knowing that the river of American steel still flows.

A Note on the Sources

Any biographer of Andrew Carnegie has to begin by looking at the Carnegie papers in the Library of Congress. There, among the business and personal documents spanning half a century, one finds letters to beggars and kings, presidents and prime ministers, philosophers and industrialists, all vibrant with the personality of their author. Unfortunately, massive as this collection is, it does not contain much of the material most important to a historian interested in Carnegie's skills as the manager of an industrial enterprise. Many such papers—for example Carnegie's correspondence with Captain Bill Jones—lie in the massive archives of United States Steel Corporation, which has not made them generally available to scholars.

Fortunately, the one investigator who gained access to the U.S. Steel collections, Joseph Frazier Wall, was a thorough, painstaking researcher, and the book he produced, *Andrew Carnegie* (New York, 1970), not only debunks many of the old myths about Carnegie, but also adds much new material to his story. An older biography, but one that somehow captures even more of the flavor of Carnegie's dynamic personality, is Burton J. Hendrick's *The Life of Andrew Carnegie* (New York, 1932). Hendrick had the advantage of being able to talk to Carnegie's widow and many of his business associates. Moreover, he wrote with a flair and energy too rarely found these days. James Howard Bridge, Carnegie's quondam secretary and general factotum, wrote a book of his own, *The Inside History of the Carnegie Steel Company* (New York, 1903). Bridge had become partisan to Frick by the time he wrote *The Inside History,* and this bias distorts the book. Bridge does give indispensable information on the development of Carnegie management, however.

Other Carnegie biographies offer much less. Bernard Alderson's *Andrew Carnegie: From Telegraph Boy to Millionaire* (London, 1902), and John K. Winkler's *Incredible Carnegie* (New York, 1931) have little more than anecdotal value. An exception of course is Carnegie's own view of his life, the *Autobiography of Andrew Carnegie* (Boston, 1920), an invaluable source, though one that must be used with extraordinary care to avoid the pitfalls of Carnegie's self-serving memory.

Secondary materials on Carnegie's life and times abound, and only a few can be mentioned here. The best single source on the Chartist movements of Carnegie's youth is F. C. Mather, *Public Order in the Age of the Chartists* (Manchester, 1959). An overview of young Carnegie's America and its economy can be found in George Rogers Taylor, *The Transportation Revolution, 1815–1860* (New York, 1968), and Edward C. Kirkland, *Industry Comes of Age* (Chicago, 1967). Both of these include detailed lists of sources. Also very helpful is Louis Hacker, *The World of Andrew Carnegie* (Philadelphia, 1968), a diffuse and sometimes infuriating book but nevertheless valuable because it reflects the dynamism and excitement of the economy Hacker studied all his life and understood so well.

The history of American management is most elaborately explored in the works of Alfred D. Chandler. *The Railroads: The Nation's First Big Business* (New York, 1965) told much of the story for the first half of the nineteenth century. The sources Chandler used are particularly helpful in placing Carnegie's railroad career in proper perspective. Chandler's successive works, *Strategy and Structure* (Boston, 1969), *Visible Hand* (Cambridge, Mass., 1977), and *Scale and Scope* (Cambridge, Mass., 1990), together have created a matchless portrait of the development of management in the United States and abroad. Recently, debunking Chandler has become a cottage industry. A leading specimen can be found in Phillip Scranton *Endless Novelty* (Princeton, N.J., 1997).

A brief but useful volume with many bibliographic references is Glenn Porter's *Rise of Big Business, 1860–1910* (New York, 1973). Some material on the development of management in antebellum rail rolling mills, the forerunners to the Edgar Thomson Works, is in Patrick G. Porter and Harold C. Livesay, *Merchants and Manufacturers* (Baltimore, 1971). Otherwise, little information has been collected in a single source. Despite its importance in the growth of the American industrial economy, the iron and steel industry has no book that provides a comprehensive history. Joseph Wall's research in the U.S. Steel papers therefore is doubly valuable, and I have relied heavily on his account.

Histories of management and industries are not the only missing ingredients for a portrait of the American economy in the nineteenth century. There is also a shortage of biographies, particularly of Carnegie's contemporaries and associates. There is none of Scott, nor of Phipps, nor anything informative about Charles Schwab. George Harvey, *Henry Clay Frick, The Man* (New York, 1936), is just slightly better than nothing. Recent additions to the Frick literature include Samuel Schreiner, *Henry Clay Frick* (New York, 1995), and Kenneth Warren, *Triumphant Capitalism* (Pittsburgh, 1996). Frederick Lewis Allen's *The Great Pierpont Morgan* (New York, 1949) is full of fun and fable, but reveals remarkably little (though doubtless all that Allen could learn) about Morgan's business career. Much less fun, but scholarly and authoritative, is Vincent Carosso's *The Morgan: Private International Bankers* (Cambridge, Massachusetts, 1987). Burton J. Hendrick and Daniel Henderson, *Louise Whitfield Carnegie* (New York, 1952), is a sympathetic portrait containing only peripheral glimpses of Carnegie the businessman. Carnegie has not escaped the tide of postmodernist humbug, as witness Alun Munslow, "Andrew Carnegie and the Discourse of Cultural Hegemony," *Journal of American Studies,* XXII (August 1988), 213–224.

In recent decades the study of labor has focused increasingly on the crucial issue of workplace control. See, for example, David Montgomery, *Workers' Control in America: Studies in the History of Work, Technology, and Labor Struggles* (New York, 1979) as well as his *The Fall of the House of Labor: The*

218 + Andrew Carnegie

Workplace, the State, American Labor Activism (New York, 1987). For the steel industry in particular, the most compelling account of labor's nineteenth-century struggles, as well as the most perceptive discussion of the working of the mills, remains David Brody's *Steelworkers in America: The Nonunion Era* (Cambridge, Massachusetts, 1960).

Homestead's history has benefited from two recent works. Paul Krause, *The Battle for Homestead* (Pittsburgh, 1992), is sympathetic to the workers, as is William Serrin, *Homestead: The Story and Tragedy of an American Steel Town* (New York, 1993).

More helpful information lies in voluminous documents of the United States Government. For example, the *Report of the Committee of the Judiciary on "Employment of Pinkerton Detectives"* (House Report #2447, 52d Cong., 2d sess., 1892–93) tells much about Homestead. For the events of the decade preceding the formation of United States Steel, the *Stanley Committee Report* (62d Cong., 2d sess., Report #1127) contains a wealth of material, much of it in Carnegie's own testimony that, like all his utterances, must be used with care.

In addition to his Stanley Committee testimony and his personal papers, Carnegie himself generated a mountain of material. As a man who had opinions on many subjects, who could afford secretarial and editorial assistance, and who exerted certain influence on publishers and editors, Carnegie wrote and published a great deal. In addition to his *Autobiography* he wrote several travel accounts such as *An American Four-in-Hand in Britain* (Boston, 1883) and *Round the World* (Garden City, 1933), which bristle with the "Star Spangled Scotsman's" patriotic enthusiasm for his adopted homeland.

More relevant for economic historians are Carnegie's lengthy expositions of his views of political economy, wealth, the virtues of the self-made man, and labor relations. These include *Triumphant Democracy* (London, 1886), and "The Advantages of Poverty," which, together with the title essay and similar gems, is in *The Gospel of Wealth and Other Timely Essays* (Cambridge, Mass., 1962), edited by Edward C. Kirkland. Two of Carnegie's more controversial pieces, "An Employer's View of the Labor Question" and "Results of the Labor Struggle," appeared in *Forum*, I, 114–125, 538–551. A myriad of other articles on subjects ranging from conservation of natural resources to a critique of the national banking system can be found in *North American Review, Outlook,* and similar journals of the day.

Carnegie's utterances also peppered the pages of contemporary newspapers. Reporters quoted him frequently; he was accessible, vain, outspoken, and iconoclastic, all qualities that made him excellent copy. Scanning the newspapers and magazines for Carnegie material also gives the reader a sense of the times in which Carnegie lived. There is, of course, a long list of scholarly works for the truly indefatigably curious. One of these works (and one which extensively considers Carnegie) is Robert G. McCloskey, *American Conservatism in the Age of Enterprise, 1865–1910* (Cambridge, Mass., 1951). An exhaustive bibliography of such works could be compiled from Wall's footnotes. None, however, captures the flavor of the past as well as two old, multivolumed warriors, Ellis Paxson Oberholtzer's *A History of the United States since the Civil War* (New York, 1917–1937), and Mark Sullivan's *Our Times, 1900–1925* (New York, 1927–1936).

Index